NO MORE EXCUSES

BE THE MAN GOD MADE YOU TO BE

TONY EVANS

Lifeway Press®
Brentwood, Tennessee

Editorial Team

Heather Hair
Writer

Reid Patton
Content Editor

David Haney
Production Editor

Jon Rodda
Art Director

Joel Polk
Editorial Team Leader

Brian Daniel
Manager, Short-Term Discipleship

Michael Kelley
Director, Discipleship and Groups Ministry

ISBN 978-1-0877-9027-5 • Item 005843170

Dewey decimal classification: 248.842
Subject headings: CHRISTIAN LIFE / MEN / CHARACTER

My deepest thanks go to Mrs. Heather Hair for her skills and insights in collaboration on this manuscript.

Scripture quotations are taken from the New American Standard Bible®, Copyright © 1960, 1962, 1963, 1968,
1971, 1972, 1973, 1975, 1977, 1995 by The Lockman Foundation. Used by permission. (www.lockman.org)

To order additional copies of this resource, write to Lifeway Resources Customer Service; 200 Powell Place, Suite
100; Brentwood, TN 37027-7707; fax 615-251-5933; call toll free 800-458-2772; order online at Lifeway.com; or
email orderentry@lifeway.com.

Printed in the United States of America

Groups Ministry Publishing • Lifeway Resources • 200 Powell Place, Suite 100 • Brentwood, TN 37027-7707

CONTENTS

About the Author 4

About The Urban Alternative 5

How to Get the Most from This Study 6

Tips for Leading a Small Group 7

Week 1
No More Hiding behind the Past 10

Week 2
No More Holding Back 26

Week 3
No More Weak Leadership 42

Week 4
No More Going through the Motions 58

Week 5
No More Compromising Your Integrity 74

Week 6
No More Sifting through the Rubble 90

Week 7
No More Half Stepping 106

Week 8
No More Standing on the Sidelines 122

D-Group Guide 138

ABOUT THE AUTHOR

DR. TONY EVANS is one of America's most respected leaders in evangelical circles. He's a pastor, a best-selling author, and a frequent speaker at Bible conferences and seminars throughout the nation. He has served as the senior pastor of Oak Cliff Bible Fellowship for more than forty years, witnessing its growth from ten people in 1976 to more than ten thousand congregants with more than one hundred ministries.

Dr. Evans also serves as the president of The Urban Alternative, a national ministry that seeks to restore hope and transform lives through the proclamation and application of God's Word. His daily radio broadcast, *The Alternative with Dr. Tony Evans,* can be heard on more than 1,300 radio outlets throughout the United States and in more than 130 countries.

Dr. Evans holds the honor of writing and publishing the first full-Bible commentary and study Bible by an African-American. A former chaplain for the Dallas Cowboys, he's currently the chaplain for the NBA's Dallas Mavericks, a team he has served for more than thirty years.

Through his local church and national ministry, Dr. Evans has set in motion a kingdom-agenda philosophy of ministry that teaches God's comprehensive rule over every area of life, as demonstrated through the individual, family, church, and society.

Dr. Evans is married to Lois, his wife and ministry partner of more than forty years. They are the proud parents of four—Chrystal, Priscilla, Anthony Jr., and Jonathan—and have a number of grandchildren.

ABOUT THE URBAN ALTERNATIVE

The Urban Alternative (TUA) is a Christian broadcast and teaching ministry founded more than thirty-five years ago by Dr. Tony Evans. TUA seeks to promote a kingdom-agenda philosophy designed to enable people to live all of life underneath the comprehensive rule of God. This is accomplished through a variety of means, including media, resources, clergy ministries, and community-impact training.

HOW TO GET THE MOST FROM THIS STUDY

This Bible-study book includes eight weeks of content for group and personal study.

GROUP SESSIONS

Regardless of what day of the week your group meets, each week of content begins with the group session. Each group session uses the following format to facilitate simple yet meaningful interaction among group members, with God's Word, and with the teaching of Dr. Evans.

START. This page includes questions to get the conversation started and to introduce the video teaching.

WATCH. This page includes key points from Dr. Evans's teaching so that participants can follow along as they watch the video.

MAN UP. This page includes questions and statements that guide the group to respond to Dr. Evans's video teaching and to relevant Bible passages.

PERSONAL STUDY

Each week provides three days of Bible study and learning activities for individual engagement between group sessions: "Hit the Streets" and two Bible studies.

HIT THE STREETS. This section highlights practical steps for taking the week's teaching and putting it into practice.

BIBLE STUDIES. These personal studies revisit stories, Scriptures, and themes Dr. Evans introduced in the videos so that men can understand and apply them on a personal level. Men should use the other days of the week to reflect on what God is teaching them and to practice putting the biblical principles into action.

D-GROUP GUIDES

In addition to the group sessions and personal studies, D-Group guides are provided at the back of this Bible-study book. These guides correspond to the eight weeks of study and are designed to be used in a smaller group of three or four men for deeper discussion and accountability. Each week's guide includes an article written by one of Dr. Evans's sons, Anthony or Jonathan, as well as a guide for smaller-group discussion. Each guide provides helpful thoughts on the week's content and suggests a few questions for discussion by and accountability among the group.

TIPS FOR LEADING A SMALL GROUP

Follow these guidelines to prepare for each group session.

PRAYERFULLY PREPARE

REVIEW. Review the weekly material and group questions ahead of time.

PRAY. Be intentional about praying for each person in the group.

Ask the Holy Spirit to work through you and the group discussion as you point to Jesus each week through God's Word.

MINIMIZE DISTRACTIONS

Create a comfortable environment. If group members are uncomfortable, they'll be distracted and therefore not engaged in the group experience. Plan ahead by considering these details, include seating, temperature, lighting, food and drink, and general cleanliness. Do everything in your ability to help people focus on what's most important: connecting with God, with the Bible, and with one another.

ENCOURAGE DISCUSSION

A good small-group experience has the following characteristics.

EVERYONE IS INCLUDED. Your goal is to foster a community in which people are welcome just as they are but encouraged to grow spiritually. Always be aware of opportunities to include any people who visit the group and to invite new people to join your group.

EVERYONE PARTICIPATES. Encourage everyone to ask questions, share responses, or read aloud.

NO ONE DOMINATES—NOT EVEN THE LEADER. Be sure that your time speaking as a leader takes up less than half of your time together as a group. Politely guide discussion if anyone dominates.

NOBODY IS RUSHED THROUGH QUESTIONS. Don't feel that a moment of silence is a bad thing. People often need time to think about their responses to questions they've just heard or to gain courage to share what God is stirring in their hearts.

INPUT IS AFFIRMED AND FOLLOWED UP. Make sure you point out something true or helpful in a response. Don't just move on. Build community with follow-up questions, asking how other people have experienced similar things or how a truth has shaped their understanding of God and the Scripture you're studying. People are less likely to speak up if they fear that you don't actually want to hear their answers or that you're looking for only a certain answer.

GOD AND HIS WORD ARE CENTRAL. Opinions and experiences can be helpful, but God has given us the truth. Trust God's Word to be the authority and God's Spirit to work in people's lives. You can't change anyone, but God can. Continually point people to the Word and to active steps of faith.

KEEP CONNECTING

Think of ways to connect with group members during the week. Participation during the group session is always improved when members spend time connecting with one another outside the group sessions. The more people are comfortable with and involved in one another's lives, the more they'll look forward to being together. When people move beyond being friendly to truly being friends who form a community, they come to each session eager to engage instead of merely attending.

Encourage group members with thoughts, commitments, or questions from the session by connecting through these communication channels:

EMAILS
TEXTS
SOCIAL MEDIA

When possible, build deeper friendships by planning or spontaneously inviting group members to join you outside your regularly scheduled group time for activities like these:

MEALS
FUN ACTIVITIES
PROJECTS AROUND YOUR HOME, CHURCH, OR COMMUNITY

Week 1
NO MORE HIDING BEHIND THE PAST

START

Welcome to group session 1 of No More Excuses.

Welcome to *No More Excuses*. In this Bible study we're going to identify and overcome the excuses men use to keep them from being the men God has called them to be. We'll begin by looking at the past.

What's an event in your past that you often think about?

Our past is made up of the good, the bad, and the ugly. Many of our experiences have been positive, but many have also been bad or painful. Painful pasts come in all shapes, sizes, and degrees of intensity. Like it or not, our past often influences our present.

What's an example of something from your past that influences the way you live in the present?

What can you do to overcome the negative influence of your past? The Bible has a lot to teach us on this subject. Let's watch session 1, in which we'll explore the life of Joseph, a man who overcame a lot of obstacles and opposition to rise to a position of great power, authority, and influence for God's purposes in the world.

Ask someone to pray before watching the video teaching.

WATCH

SESSION 1 Video. *To access the teaching sessions,*
use the instructions in the back of your Bible study book.

God does not want us to make excuses for the failures in our lives. He wants us to take responsibility.

We can no longer hide behind the past. We can no longer let yesterday define us.

We men need God to deliver us from yesterday because too many of us are chained to yesterday.

God wants to deliver men from the hostage taking the enemy has done in our lives so that we're able to blaze into our future, getting rid of the limp and the excuse and not being held hostage to the past.

God can take your yesterday and turn it into an awesome tomorrow.

Forgiving does not mean you don't remember it happened. It means you're no longer seeking revenge because it happened.

God can take the mess of yesterday and turn it into the miracle of tomorrow. He can take the pain of the past and turn it into the productivity of the future. He can take the limp and give you life.

MAN UP

Use the following questions to discuss the video teaching.

Read Genesis 50:20.

Joseph embraced his past because he recognized that God had used it to turn around his present and give him a pleasurable, productive future. We often hear that hindsight is always 20/20. Joseph made this statement in a season of his life during which he lived out the fulfillment of God's plan for him and the nation of Israel. You could say he was already in the winner's circle. But God has called us to live according to this truth even when we haven't yet seen Him turn our circumstances around. He asks us to do that by faith.

> **What are some hindrances to living in the truth of Genesis 50:20 before we've seen God turn our situation around? An example might be doubt.**

> **What are some benefits of embracing the truth of Genesis 50:20 in full faith? An example might be greater confidence. Identify other benefits.**

In sports if a player fails to make a kick, catch, tackle, or prevent a completed pass, the player sometimes gets up with a limp. At times that limp reflects a real injury, like the one Sebastian Janikowski experienced in the Cowboys-Seahawks wild-card game in January 2019. Following a missed field goal, Janikowski was out for the rest of the game because of a torn hamstring. But sometimes a player gets up and limps when nothing is wrong at all. A player uses that kind of limp, what I call a loser's limp, to imply that he failed because of an injury, not through any fault of his own.

The limp is an excuse. It implies that if the player had been at full capacity, he would have been successful. It's meant to draw attention away from the failure of the present by directing that attention to an excuse that preceded it.

> **In what ways might men use this loser's limp excuse in everyday life?**

On the video Dr. Evans said, "God does not want us to make excuses for the failures in our lives. He wants us to take responsibility and ownership. ... That means that we can no longer hide behind the past. We can no longer let yesterday define us." Injury or not, painful past or not, God opposes the use of negative situations in our lives as excuses for personal failures. We're to own our failures, get up, and move forward.

What does it look like to own a personal setback or challenge in the present instead of making an excuse for it?

Dr. Evans used the example of an enormous adult elephant staying chained to a small stake due to its memory of the past. As a younger, smaller elephant, it couldn't pull away from the stake. As an adult, it could get loose, but the memory of the past keeps the strong elephant chained because it believes it can't break free.

Name common mindsets that hold men back from fully living out their strength and biblical authority.

All of us have gone through difficult experiences. Joseph's example is poignant but not isolated. Joseph got through those days by recognizing that God was with him. God is with you as well. And He was with you during the challenging experiences in your past.

Dr. Evans said Joseph had to forgive yesterday. This meant no longer seeking revenge, sulking, or staring at the past but trusting that God knew how to turn it around for good.

Do you need to forgive someone or something? It might even be yourself. Identify benefits of forgiveness that you learned from the video teaching.

PRAYER

Close the session with prayer.

Father, in a world full of excuses, You've asked us to rise above them and
live with personal responsibility and ownership. Help each of us identify
past hurts and experiences we need to let go of, forgive, and see in the
light of Your power and purpose. Help us live as men without excuses
as we trust in Your ability to transform our lives. In Christ's name, amen.

HIT THE STREETS

Three Steps to Winning the Race

Every Thanksgiving my family and I take part in what's known as the Turkey Trot. This 5K run/walk brings thousands of people together with the goal of raising funds for the Dallas YMCA. In this race, finishing is winning because all proceeds go to a good cause. But not so for most races. Most races award a first-place finisher with a medal, trophy, jacket, or another symbol of victory. In those races, coming in fifth, tenth, or one-hundredth is never the goal. Athletes train and compete in order to come in first.

Paul pictured the Christian life as a race. He wrote:

> *Do you not know that those who run in a race all run, but only one receives the prize? Run in such a way that you may win.*
> 1 CORINTHIANS 9:24

Men, I want to challenge you to develop a passion to be a winner for God. Following these three strategic steps can help you accomplish your goals.

1. Go for the Gold

A nice jogging suit doesn't make you a runner, just as wearing a football jersey doesn't make you an NFL player. To go for the gold, you need to do more than be a part of the pack. Never settle for simply getting on the field or in the race. Yet even the glory of a thrilling win on the field will pass. The glory God has for all who know Him is eternal and unfading. One day God is going to reward you for what you do for Him. Because of the nature of that reward, you pursue "the upward call of God in Christ Jesus" (Phil. 3:14) with all you have. Living a life filled with excuses keeps you from pursing the finish line with a fervor and intensity befitting the stakes of your eternal race.

2. Keep Your Eye on the Prize

Athletes who compete take part in strict training. They do this in order to get the prize. Strict training and hard work are just that—hard. They're disciplines you have to make yourself do. Unless you stay focused on the *why* behind the *what,* you might quit.

We have an Olympic gold medalist who attends the church where I pastor. I've known her since she was a kid. The hours, days, weeks, and months she put into preparing for the Olympics were possible only because she kept her eye on the prize. Every decision she made in the years leading up to her gold medal was influenced by that one pursuit. We, as kingdom men, ought to pursue God's eternal prize with no less effort.

Kingdom men train daily in godliness. They invest in the eternal. They seek to spend time with the Lord in prayer and Bible study, they serve others, and give sacrificially of themselves to the cause of the kingdom.

3. Remove Distractions

The writer of Hebrews expressed the last step this way:

> *Let us also lay aside every encumbrance*
> *and the sin which so easily entangles us.*
> HEBREWS 12:1

What's distracting you? In what ways are you spending your time on things that aren't of eternal value? Get rid of it. Stop watching it. Stop talking to them. Stop going there. Whatever stands in the way of fully living out and gaining the victory ought to have no place in your life.

Go for the gold; never settle. Keep your eye on the prize set before you. Remove the distractions holding you back. Follow these three steps, and you'll live as a victorious kingdom man.

If You're Not Dead, God's Not Done

Various passages in the Bible picture the Christian life as a race or other athletic competition (see 1 Tim. 4:7-8; Gal. 5:7; Heb. 12:1; Jas. 1:12). Parallels abound. Both require attention and effort. Both require self-denial and perseverance. Both have a clearly defined finish line we strive for. The finish line of this study is to become a kingdom man—a man who places himself under God's rulership and submits his life to the lordship of Jesus Christ. A kingdom man lives according to God's rule. Now that we have a goal in mind, we'll begin making strides toward the finish line.

Unlike athletic competition, the race for the Christian lasts a lifetime. If you're not dead yet, you aren't finished yet. You still have time to push forward in the race and win. You may be coming to the starting blocks with regrets over personal, family, or spiritual failure. You may have stumbled coming out of the blocks. You may have tripped during the race. You may even be starting the race a little late, but God can help you make up for lost time. He can help you pick up speed in the last half of the race and cover more ground in less time than the average runner.

Read the following verse and answer the questions.

I am confident of this very thing, that He who began a good work in you will perfect it until the day of Christ Jesus.
PHILIPPIANS 1:6

What confidence comes from knowing that God began and will complete the work in your life?

Our relationship with God begins with God. Paul was saying that what God starts, He finishes. What God initiates, He completes. God wants us to be involved in His mission in the world to make Himself known by making His people more like His Son. He always helps us finish. Sometimes it may appear that God is doing nothing and everything is up to us. Yet God routinely works behind the scenes to lead us toward the finish line.

How do you rest in the confidence that God will carry out His work in your life from start to finish? How should this assurance influence your emotions, prayers, and actions?

Paul knew how to persevere. He knew how to let go of the past. Paul had a shady past. He persecuted and oppressed the church. But one day Jesus met him on the road to Damascus. That encounter changed Paul's life. He knew the wisdom of forgetting failures and even successes. He wrote about it in Philippians 3. Paul pressed on:

Brethren, I do not regard myself as having laid hold of it yet; but one thing I do: forgetting what lies behind and reaching forward to what lies ahead ...
PHILIPPIANS 3:13

What excuses in failures from you past are you holding on to?

You may not be able to completely forget your past, but in what ways can you follow Paul's example of "forgetting what lies behind" and look forward to what's ahead?

Paul has a kingdom-man attitude. He let go of the things that were behind him. His eyes were straight ahead, focused on the goal. Runners don't win a race looking backward. They have to keep their eyes on the finish line. You can't change yesterday, but you can do a lot about what happens tomorrow. Don't let other people stop you from running for God. Don't let other people distract you from seeking His approval.

NO MORE EXCUSES

The truth is that if you know Jesus, you already have God's approval. When you believed the gospel, God exchanged all the sin in your past, present, and future for the perfect life of His Son. You're now in Christ, so when God sees you, He doesn't see your past; He sees Jesus' perfect record. God isn't concerned about your past failures; however, He has an unmistakable, amazing way of using even failure to bring about success.

Often we spend too much time thinking about what other people think about us and allow it to hold us back. Why is it important to focus only on God and His view of you instead of what others think about you?

God has a purpose for your life, a destiny for you to live out, a plan that He uniquely created you to fulfill. You advance toward that goal by focusing each day on aligning your thoughts, attitudes, and behavior with His Word and His will. Be faithful in the small things, and He will put you in charge of many things (see Matt. 25:21). If you drop a pass or miss a tackle, don't blame others or yourself. Don't get sidelined for a play. Get back up; admit your failure to God, trusting in His provision for your forgiveness (the Bible calls this step repentance); let it go; and move forward in the knowledge that your past doesn't define you. Because you're accepted and forgiven, you're living under God's approval.

Living in God's approval allows us to bear spiritual fruit, which is the outward evidence that we're being inwardly changed by God's work in our lives. For example, when a man lifts weights, the hours in the gym show up as fruit in the body as muscles begin to develop and his body responds to the difficulties it has endured. Similarly, spiritual sculpting takes place when you let go of your past and take responsibility for your sins and your spiritual development. Fruit can include greater patience, tolerance, self-control, love, diligence, leadership, wisdom, grace, and a myriad of other traits and actions that lead to eternal rewards.

Why would an unhealthy fixation on our past keep us from bearing fruit in the present?

Why is it important that we bear fruit after repenting of sin? What does it signify if we don't?

For Paul, bearing fruit was rooted in self-control. He tells us:

> *Everyone who competes in the games exercises self-control*
> *in all things. They then do it to receive a perishable wreath,*
> *but we an imperishable. Therefore I run in such a way, as*
> *not without aim; I box in such a way, as not beating the air;*
> *but I discipline my body and make it my slave, so that, after*
> *I have preached to others, I myself will not be disqualified.*
> 1 CORINTHIANS 9:25-27

The best athletes exhibit self-control. The Greek word Paul used for *self-control* in verse 25 referred to athletes in his day who abstained from unhealthy food, wine, and sex prior to competition. These athletes understood the need for their bodies to be at full capacity for victory. They were willing to invest in themselves to win the prize set before them.

The prize in the Christian life is in the future. Hiding behind the past is harmful because it focuses our attention in the wrong place. It causes us to feel shame and guilt over past failings instead of resting in the approval we have in Jesus and in the confidence that comes from knowing He will finish the work He began. We need to exercise diligence and self-control to let go of the past.

What's one area of your life in which you're willing to exercise self-control in order to have a greater capacity for spiritual focus and commitment?

PRAY

Pray about your personal commitment to God and His expression
of greatness through you. Ask Him to give you a glimpse of His plans
for your future and to inspire you on your path of spiritual development.
Ask for His help in reducing distractions that keep you from fully
pursuing Him. Thank Him for the work He has begun in your life
and ask Him to increase your faith and bring it to completion.

BIBLE STUDY 2
Crown Me

Ever played checkers? It's a fun game. Once you're able to move a checker to the other side of the board, you get to say, "Crown me." That means your checker is rewarded with all of the rights and privileges of a king. Now that you're wearing a crown, movement and mastery come more easily, and your odds of winning go up.

The kingdom life comes with its own rewards as well. When you obtain these, either in time or in eternity, you're entitled to all of the rights and privileges they supply. Scripture calls them crowns. Today we'll look at five of them.

As a kingdom man, you have all it takes to obtain each of these crowns. You just need to pursue them the way God has instructed. But I have to point out that it won't be easy. Unlike compliments in our culture, crowns don't come cheap. The Greek word used for *crown* is *stephanos*. It means "badge of royalty." The crowns the Bible describes are different from earthly treasure, which is subject to decay and corruption.

Read Jesus' words in Matthew 6:19-21.

Describe the difference between treasure on earth and treasure in heaven.

THE CROWN OF MASTERY. The first crown is the crown of mastery, the reward for faithful obedience, which we've already read about in 1 Corinthians 9:24-25. A man wins this crown by committing to discipline himself in order to compete successfully. No one ever becomes good at anything without disciplining himself. Maybe you've heard of the ten-thousand-hour rule that Malcolm Gladwell made famous.[1] The principle is that it requires ten thousand hours of doing something again and again until you master it. Although ten thousand hours may not be the exact requirement, the point is that consistency creates competency, and competency leads to mastery. You must be consistent in your spiritual walk and development over a long period of time in order to win this crown.

Read 1 Corinthians 9:24-25. How can you become more consistent in your spiritual development?

We develop spiritually by engaging in spiritual disciples like Bible reading, prayer, fasting, giving, serving, and others. Which of these would be most beneficial for you? When will you engage in them?

THE CROWN OF REJOICING. First Thessalonians 2:19 tells us about our next crown—the crown of rejoicing. This crown is associated with faithfulness in the work of evangelism. God will honor men who made winning others to Christ the passion of their lives. It's good for us as kingdom men to stop regularly and take inventory of how often we share the gospel with others.

Read 1 Thessalonians 2:19. When was the most recent time you led someone to Christ or shared the gospel?

With whom could you share your faith this week? How are you building that relationship?

THE CROWN OF GLORY. The third crown is the crown of glory, given for faithfulness in discipleship. The apostle Peter described this crown in 1 Peter 5:2-4. The idea of discipling is to lead someone in such a way that he desires to follow you in your Christian walk. According to Peter, men who lead others to maturity in Christ will be rewarded. They'll be put in God's hall of fame. The word *glory* used in this passage means "to put something on display."

NO MORE EXCUSES

I visited the NFL headquarters in New York when we filmed for the feature documentary *Kingdom Men Rising*. On one of the upper floors was a magnificent display cabinet running the length of the room. Behind glass was displayed each Super Bowl ring going back to the beginning of the game. Also displayed was the Lombardi Trophy. It was a sight to see! Although these treasures will fade one day, the display case of your discipleship in eternity will last forever. If you're a man who has discipled many others, people will see your rewards in heaven and say, "Wow!"

Read 1 Peter 5:2-4. Who has discipled you? What did you learn from them?

What are some ways discipling can take place?

THE CROWN OF LIFE. The risen Christ told the church in Smyrna about this crown.

Read Revelation 2:10.

Some men seem to go from one trial to another. God says your hardship doesn't go unnoticed in heaven. When you endure, when you refuse to throw in the towel and make excuses, God has a crown waiting for you. If you hang in there through suffering, knowing God is working His purposes in your life even if you don't know exactly all He's doing, you'll receive this crown.

Identify times in your life when you've thrown in the towel because it got too hard.

Now repent and make a plan to begin pursuing Christ's purpose for you as a man in this area of your life. If you can't recall giving up, thank God for His faithfulness in seeing you through difficult times and ask Him to give you strength to continue.

THE CROWN OF RIGHTEOUSNESS. The crown of righteousness is given for faithfulness in ministry. Described in 2 Timothy 4:7-8, it comes through keeping the faith all the way to the end.

The good news about all five of these crowns is that you don't have to know a special secret to qualify for them. They aren't just for supersaints. Receiving them is a matter of everyday, consistent faithfulness, of getting up every morning and saying, "Lord, I give You my life today as a kingdom man. I want to obey You, to love my wife and children, and to honor You in everything I say and do."

It's important for us to realize that these crowns await us in the future. However, to receive them, we must be faithful in the present. Continuing to hide behind our past will keep us from living in the present and from looking toward the future. All of these crowns are attainable as Christ works in and through your life. He's the goal; He awards us these crowns as we faithfully pursue Him.

> **Read 2 Timothy 4:7-8. How does the hope of a future reward in heaven help us remain faithful in the present? Why does faithfulness require us to let go of our past?**

> **How does knowing that the crowns come as we faithfully pursue Christ keep you from feeling that you need to perform for God?**

PRAY

Pray and commit your day, week, and year to Christ. Submit to Him and ask Him to help you pursue Him with all your heart, soul, mind and strength.

1. Malcolm Gladwell, *Outliers: The Story of Success* (Boston: Little, Brown, 2011).

Week 2
NO MORE HOLDING BACK

START

Welcome to group session 2 of No More Excuses.

Last week we recalled events from our past that keep us from moving forward to become the kingdom men God is calling us to be.

When did you find that you're most prone to dwell in the past?

This week we're going to be encouraged to stop holding back and take responsibility. When a football team gathers in a circle before a game on its home field, one phrase always comes out: "This is our house! Dominate!" In this way the team declares its ownership over the game because it owns the space in which the game will take place. This mindset often propels the team to a victory even though it may not be favored to win.

Define the term *dominate* in your own words.

Give a positive example of what it means to dominate.

God has given you a sphere of influence that belongs to you for the purpose of owning and exercising dominion over that realm (see Gen. 1:28).

In fact, God has given each man an area of influence, whether in his family or at work, as well as in his personal life, emotions, and development. This week's teaching highlights an episode from Elisha's ministry and issues a call for you to live boldly while overcoming any efforts the enemy may use to hold you back.

Ask someone to pray before watching the video teaching.

WATCH

SESSION 2 Video. *To access the teaching sessions,*
use the instructions in the back of your Bible study book.

God is calling on men to recognize the divine authority that has been given to them by heaven for them to execute on earth.

Claim a victory you do not yet see and you do not yet have, but because you handed it off to the Victor, you're starting in a different place.

We're going to hand the ball off to God, but we're going to do what we need to do to make sure we are participants in the solution God wants to bring.

God is calling men to reach high to heaven, but He's also calling them to touch low on earth and implement what you're believing God to do.

God works out things in the spiritual before He reveals them in the physical.

If you've dropped some balls in the first half, this is the time to get up and not hold back.

Far too many men are waiting on God when God is waiting on us.

God has given you equipment to handle the attacks that come, the warfare that is coming against you, the pain you're experiencing, the defeats you've had.

I'm going to give God everything I've got because I'm going to give God something to work with.

When you do it God's way and start with your spiritual commitment first, He brings heaven's pleasure into your pain, into your failure, into your frustrations, into your future.

The only time you stop is when God stops you, not when you stop yourself.

MAN UP

Use the following questions to discuss the video teaching.

Read the following verse together.

Elisha said to him, "Take a bow and arrows."
So he took a bow and arrows.
2 KINGS 13:15

As the prophet Elisha was dying, the king of Israel, Joash, was distraught. Joash was acting like a frightened child instead of a confident king. Elisha commanded the king to pick up the bow and arrow and shoot arrows to mark God's victory. Joash shot three arrows and then stopped. Elisha confronted Joash's lack of confidence. He could have shot five or six arrows but had decided to stop with three.

God is calling on men to pick up the tools He has given them and use them. God is raising up a generation of men who won't hold back. He wants us to have a dominant spirit. That doesn't mean to dominate in an illegitimate way but rather to recognize the divine authority given to us by heaven in order to execute God's purposes on earth. We've been assigned to bring heaven's rule into history.

How could a negative understanding of dominance reduce or remove many men's desire to boldly live out their faith?

What did Joash miss by holding back? What have you missed?

In the 2018–19 NFL season two players left games at halftime. The Bills' Vontae Davis left and quit. The Steelers' Antonio Brown left, indicating that he wanted to be traded. On the video Dr. Evans used the example of leaving the game midway and going into the stands to describe men who hold back from living out their kingdom calling. Far too many men take initiative, only to throw in the towel midway when emotions, relationships, or finances become difficult. Examples could include pursuing a dream, investing in marriage, discipling others, mentoring, growing in Christ, praying, and other areas of life.

What types of challenges contribute to a man's decision to throw in the towel?

On the video Dr. Evans said, "Worse than leaving the fields and going up into the stands, men have decided to become spectators so that somebody else can solve the problem. Yet God has created them to get on the field and to call this His house."

What does it look like for men to call creation God's house? Give an example in each of these areas of a man's everyday life: personal life, family, church, community, and nation.

The biblical account of Elisha's instruction for King Joash to shoot all of his arrows out the window came with a unique twist. That twist involved the prophet's laying his hands on the king's hands (see 2 Kings 13:16). This formal, public display of assistance served as a reminder to the king where his true power originated and where he would find his victory. God supplied power to the king to the extent that the king obeyed and relied on God.

How might men seek to gain their own victories in life without relying on God's power or without completely obeying His will?

The king's half-hearted obedience in shooting only three arrows into the ground disqualified him from complete victory over his enemy. The king held back some of his resources instead of trusting God's word through the prophet in complete faith. Total obedience brings about total victory. Holding back only hurts yourself.

How do we sometimes rationalize holding back rather than living boldly with total obedience and complete faith?

PRAYER

Close the session with prayer.

Father, make us men who hold nothing back. Let us leave our all on the field
of our pursuits for Your kingdom. We want to trust You fully, follow You
completely, and watch You gain victories in our lives. Put us in the game and
let us live out the entirety of Your purposes for us. In Christ's name, amen.

HIT THE STREETS

Go Get It!

God has given us more than five thousand promises in Scripture, but He's not going to force anyone to live in the victory of His fulfilled promises. You have to go get them. When the people of Israel entered the promised land, God promised their leader, Joshua, that He would be given any piece of land where his foot walked (see Josh. 1:3), but he had to go get it. He couldn't stand where he was and simply claim victory over all of his enemies.

Here are four key principles for claiming the promises God has made.

1. Leave the Past Behind

Learn from yesterday; don't live in it. As Joshua set out to take the Israelites on a military conquest across enormous geographical areas, he had to let go of Moses as the leader and commander. As we see in Joshua 1:1-2, Moses had died. The miracles Moses had performed for the Israelite people were in the past. God would use a new man and a new plan to secure the nation's victories moving forward. Embracing that truth was critical for their progress.

2. Seize Your Spiritual Inheritance

Joshua had to take steps of faith to secure the promises God had made. God placed a condition on receiving His victories. Joshua had to place the sole of his foot where he might normally have been afraid to do so. Doing so required faith. Passively waiting for God to dump your spiritual promises onto you isn't the way God operates. You have to go after them.

3. Focus on God, Not People

God promised Joshua:

> *No man will be able to stand before you all the days*
> *of your life. Just as I have been with Moses, I will*
> *be with you; I will not fail you or forsake you.*
> JOSHUA 1:5

No doubt Joshua faced oversized, overpowering enemies as he sought to gain military victories and conquer the promised land. But God assured him of victory. If Joshua had focused on the people in his way, he might have cowered in fear. Likewise, when you direct your focus on God and His assuring Word, you can reduce fear and doubt in your life. Keep your eyes on your Source and only on your Source.

4. Stay Tethered to God's Word

A critical element in Joshua's conquests was his consistency in staying tied to God's Word. God instructed him:

> *Only be strong and very courageous; be careful to*
> *do according to all the law which Moses My servant*
> *commanded you; do not turn from it to the right or to*
> *the left, so that you may have success wherever you go.*
> JOSHUA 1:7

God's Word gives wisdom on what to do, when to do it, and how to gain spiritual victories in the midst of physical limitations or obstacles. Men, as you move forward in life, meditate on and apply the truths of Scripture, and you'll gain insight for accomplishing all God has in store for you.

BIBLE STUDY 1
The Fixer-Upper

Men like to fix things. We see a problem, analyze it, and seek to fix it. In fact, we like to fix things so much that our wives often complain that we're trying to fix what they're talking about rather than simply listening. Sometimes our wives just want us to listen. But men were created to conquer, correct, fix, redeem, and restore. It's what we do.

However, no one can fix things like God. God has as many methods of fixing things as there are stars in the sky. He's the great unfigureoutable God. He knows how to turn upside-down conditions right side up again. He can turn around job situations on a dime and heal wounds that have festered for years. The problem comes when we try to figure out how He's going to bring about change or when we resist His method for doing it. Issues arise when we think we need to help God or try to fix what He's already fixing Himself.

Read Joshua 3:1-13 before answering the following questions.

What did God promise Joshua He would do when the priests stood in the water?

What kind of faith must it have taken for the priests to obey Joshua's orders as they crossed the Jordan? What would have happened if they had held back?

Joshua's directions must have been shocking to the priests. The Bible doesn't tell us, but they may have been tempted to hold back. Holding back happens when we fail to trust God and His plans. We falsely believe that because His plans don't make sense to us, they don't make sense at all. Holding back keeps us from experiencing all God has for us. Our best moments happen when we refuse to hold back and begin taking steps of faith.

In Joshua 3 it wasn't immediately clear that God would part the Jordan by faith. God rarely tells us the *how* because He wants us to walk by faith and not by sight. In addition, if God told us the *how,* we might argue with Him. After all, few of us have the faith of Joshua, who was willing to walk around an enemy's walled city for seven days, open and vulnerable to attack (see chap. 6). Most of us would have asked God if He had gotten enough sleep the night before and then proposed an alternative plan of attack. Joshua had the faith to obey God because he had witnessed God's unusual activity in his life time and time again. He didn't withhold his obedience. Instead, he trusted God and moved in faith.

Has God ever asked you to do something that didn't make sense? What was the result? How does this experience keep you from holding back in the future?

Hebrews 11:1 tells us that faith is "the conviction of things not seen." What does it mean to be convicted of or convinced of things you haven't yet seen?

How should this conviction affect your choices?

As a pastor, I'm regularly asked by men in difficult situations how God will show up and transform their challenge. My answer is always the same: "I don't know, but I know this: when God tells you to cross the Jordan, you'd better start walking and let Him work it out."

As we read in the biblical accounts, God rarely starts working out a dilemma until He sees you do what He has asked you to do. God responds when you walk by faith, not when you wish by faith. You can't exercise faith in your easy chair. Your easy chair might be good for watching football, but it doesn't take you anywhere. Your easy chair is comfortable, but far too many men are satisfied with being comfortable.

Describe the difference between talking by faith and walking by faith.

Why is it important to take steps of faith when God urges you to?

We're creatures of habit. We have routines we like to follow. If we find a successful way to do something, we often continue it, even if it doesn't work the second time around. Long-term success requires adapting and changing. NFL coaches who don't know how to make changes in their approaches at halftime are often not career-winning coaches. In fact, the teams that win the most are the ones that adapt the most to the opponents they face and the tactics used. Likewise, God isn't a "Push, play, and go" kind of God. He varies His approach based on the circumstances and personalities of the moment.

Read the following verses.

> *David inquired of the LORD, saying, "Shall I go up against the Philistines? Will You give them into my hand?" And the LORD said to David, "Go up, for I will certainly give the Philistines into your hand."*
> 2 SAMUEL 5:19

> *When David inquired of the LORD, He said, "You shall not go directly up; circle around behind them and come at them in front of the balsam trees."*
> 2 SAMUEL 5:23

Describe the difference in approach between the two battle plans.

God is anything but predictable. He may lead you one way in a situation and a totally different way in a similar situation. Though the variables may not have changed, God will choose an alternative approach.

In the first battle David was to pursue the enemy head-on. In the second round David was to wait until he heard the breeze blowing in the trees (see v. 24). I imagine that wasn't a strategy David would have learned at the academy. This example illustrates why it's critical to stay close to God, keeping the communication channels open; your heart, mind, and body pure; and your sins regularly repented of so that you can hear what He has to say.

Why is it important to listen closely to God's leading and not assume He's asking you to use the same tactic over and over again?

What step of faith is God asking you to take that you've been delaying? What would it look like to walk in faith instead of holding back in this situation?

How will you cultivate your sensitivity to God and His leading this week?

PRAY

Pray about an area of your life or in your sphere of influence that you feel needs to be fixed. Ask God to replace your thinking on how to fix it with His. Then ask Him to give you courage to take steps of faith in doing what He has asked. Invite Him to amaze you with His involvement and victory in this specific situation.

BIBLE STUDY 2
Let Go

When God called people to do something spectacular in the Bible, the deeds He called them to do were typically larger than themselves. He called Abraham to be a mighty nation. He called David to single-handedly defeat someone twice his size with a stone. He called Moses to part the Red Sea. Often you'll know it's God who's asking you to do something if it's something you can't do on your own. In fact, you can't discover how big God is unless your need is something bigger than you can handle. And when God accomplishes what you never could have done on your own, only He gets the glory. But to see God work this way, you have to let go of your strategy, skills, and successes and tap into His.

Why is it spiritually dangerous to rely too much on your past achievements or victories when you face new battles?

Moses delivered his people from slavery. He led them through treacherous terrain. He performed miracles in God's name. But he never made it into the promised land. Seems harsh, doesn't it? Not really. Moses had been used so much by God that he started doing what too many men do. He started believing the headlines and the social-media comments. Then he took matters into his own hands, and as a result, he had to pay the price.

Read about the two instances when God brought water from a rock during Moses' leadership of the Israelites. These are found in Exodus 17:6 and Numbers 20:8-12.

What differences do you see between God's instructions in these instances? Why were those differences important?

Moses may have reveled in the majesty of his own involvement the first time God had used him to bring water from a rock. Maybe he had a flair for the dramatic by this point. Whatever the case, he disobeyed God the second time and refused to let go of his ego. He struck the rock instead of simply speaking to it. As a result, Moses lost the opportunity to complete his own legacy. His pride caused him to disobey God. As a result, he lost his inheritance.

Why does ego sometimes get in the way of total obedience to God?

In what ways does our contemporary culture feed men's egos? Examples might be public awareness through digital platforms and awards.

A healthy identity and self-esteem are important in life. When you're rooted and grounded in Christ, you should feel confident and assured of what He can do both in and through you. But there's a fine line between healthy self-esteem and an overinflated ego. Once you cross that line, you may be tempted to toss a little of your own worldly wisdom into God's solution to your situation. Embracing worldly wisdom causes you to hold back from fully obeying God because you foolishly believe you can do it on your own.

Have you ever found yourself overwhelmed by a situation, and there seemed to be no earthly solution? What did you do?

As a pastor, I've never witnessed a time when men seemed to be fighting as many battles as they are today. And too many are losing. Whether in their families, finances, careers, health, pornography, debt, addictions, loneliness, or other overwhelming struggles, many men today are fighting a losing battle against sin. Concerned about the attacks they're facing, they go to God for His wisdom and His strategy. And they apply it. But only some of it.

NO MORE EXCUSES

Ego and vulnerability can cause a man to hold back and fall short of all God has for him. Men like to know the end at the beginning. Trusting God means we must admit we don't know and control everything. Not holding back can feel risky for men, so many men quit too early, thinking maybe God won't notice they're holding back.

What are some ways we might hold back from total obedience to God?

What would it look like for you to go all in with God in a particular area of your life? List three specific details you would need to adjust, let go of, or adopt. Then pause and ask God to help you make these changes.

1.

2.

3.

Men, the promises of God are true. But rarely do God's promises arrive apart from your participation. Likewise, the level of your participation affects the experience of the promise.

We all face challenges and problems that are too big for us on our own. I imagine that whatever you might be facing is real as well and that it's also big. It could be a job situation, a financial situation, or a moral situation. But when God gives you His perspective on what He wants you to do, don't hold back. Don't quit. Don't merge what He says with what your friends say, what you hear on talk radio and podcasts, or even your own ideas. The answer is already in your hands: complete, total obedience to what He asks you to do. Too many men are making too many excuses for why they can't lead well, love well, or serve well. God wants you to walk in the power of the promises He has given you.

What has God called you to do that's bigger than you?

In what way does God want to you to approach and overcome the obstacles that keep you from doing it?

God won't force your victory on you. You have to let go and go get it. You have to go win it. You have to go earn it, based on what God has revealed to you through His Word and through the confirmation of His Spirit. That is, unless you're satisfied with living in defeat or with only partial victories.

Few men have ever laid claim to their legitimate authority and their victory, because few men have wholeheartedly embraced God's promises, combined with their fulfillment of their own responsibilities. Few men step forward in faith. Far too many would rather make excuses.

What kind of pursuits do men mistake for real purpose? How do those lead us to hold back from pursuing God's purpose for our lives?

Men run on empty because they hold back from giving their best to God. Pursuing success though position, power, and possessions often camouflages a misguided purpose. But position, power, and possessions don't last. What lasts is what's done in obedience to the King of kings and the Ruler over all.

What do you need to let go of to walk in faith?

PRAY

Pray for the courage you need to let go of everything that holds you back from fulling experiencing and actualizing the victories that are yours in Jesus Christ. Ask God to reveal to you anything that stands between you and those victories. Give Him praise ahead of time for what He's about to do in your life.

Week 3
NO MORE WEAK WEAK LEADERSHIP

START

Welcome to group session 3 of No More Excuses.

Last week we recognized the value of embracing leadership and exercising ownership and dominion in our responsibilities.

In what area of responsibility did you feel convicted to begin exercising more ownership?

Once the NFL regular season ends, teams decide which coaches they'll keep and which ones have to clean out their offices. Every year Black Monday, as it's called, sends coaches packing. Not because any coach dropped a pass or missed a field goal. Not because a coach couldn't connect with his receivers or make a block. No, the coaches are fired because the players under their leadership didn't perform in a way that met the owners' expectations. Leadership stretches far beyond you.

Why did God look for Adam even though it was Eve who first ate the fruit?

In what ways are leaders accountable for the people under their care and supervision?

In this week's study we'll explore God's design for a man's leadership. We'll also examine the consequences poor leadership can have on a man's legacy. God has a definite design in mind for strong leaders, and He has created men to live out that design as their destinies.

Ask someone to pray before watching the video teaching.

WATCH

SESSION 3 Video. *To access the teaching sessions,*
use the instructions in the back of your Bible study book.

Since God is the manufacturer, He should be the One who defines what a man is and who a man truly is to be.

At the core of a definition of a man and his leadership responsibility is that he is responsible, even if he's not to blame.

God created man before he created woman because man was to be the foundation not only for the family but for the culture.

It's possible to be a male by gender but not a man by responsibility, leadership, and function.

God wants to rule over every male so that they become a man, and He wants to be in intimate relationship with every male so that we understand that God is a God not just of overseeing but of intimacy.

Every man is to be under divine authority, and when we rebel against that, our world will collapse.

I get to take what God brings, assign to it a meaning, an identity, and a destiny. I get to exercise kingdom authority by the King's permission.

If you're going to be a real man, you have to accept accountability to be under God.

In your personal relationship to Jesus Christ, God wants to grab you and pull you back into the garden of spiritual responsibility, of spiritual identity, of spiritual authority. He wants to give you back what Satan has robbed you of.

MAN UP

Use the following questions to discuss the video teaching.

Read the following verse together.

> *I want you to understand that Christ is the head of every man, and the man is the head of a woman, and God is the head of Christ.*
> 1 CORINTHIANS 11:3

This verse describes a chain of command. It reveals a hierarchy that, when followed, ushers in authority, peace, and spiritual power. Unfortunately, far too many men focus on the latter part of the verse instead of the former. When men complain to me, as their pastor, that their wives aren't submitting to their headship, one of the first questions I ask is whether they're submitting to Christ. It starts there.

What does submitting to Christ look like in practical, everyday actions?

When you build a house, you start by laying the foundation. Everything that's placed on the structure of that foundation depends on the stability of the structure itself. If the foundation shifts, cracks will appear on the walls. If the foundation crumbles, the result might be broken pipes or a sewage leak. The foundation determines the strength of all that rests on it.

God created men to serve as the foundation of their homes, churches, and communities. Strong leadership by men provides stability for the people underneath them. Weak, fractured leadership leads to broken lives all around them. Strong leaders model the leadership of Christ, who laid down His life to serve the church (see Mark 10:45; Eph. 5:25). Strong leaders seek the benefit of all under their care. That's a foundation you can trust.

Describe some ways men can live as strong leaders in their homes, churches, and communities.

On the video Dr. Evans said, "It's possible to be a male by gender but not a man by responsibility, leadership, and function." One way Satan seeks to disarm God's advancement of His kingdom agenda on earth is to downplay the need for male leadership. But strong male leadership is essential to carrying out God's rule.

What does it look like to be a male by gender but not a man by responsibility, leadership, and function?

When Adam hid from God in the garden and sought to cover himself with leaves, he was using gifts from God to hide behind. After all, God had provided the vegetation for Adam's use. We do the same thing today. Although the gifts we hide behind might not be clothes sewn with leaves, they might include our ability to talk ourselves out of a corner, our innate business mind, our athletic skills, or our God-given blessings. Using our gifts and blessings to advance God's kingdom fulfills the calling of a kingdom man. But hiding behind them to say, "Hey, I'm not so bad after all," as Adam did, is an effort to avoid taking responsibility. Rather than hide, I want to encourage you to rise to the calling of strong leadership that God has given to you. The past no longer controls you. You can lead well, starting today.

In what ways might men attempt to hide behind their blessings to give the outward appearance that they're strong spiritual leaders?

What specific, practical steps can you take this week to live according to God's standard of leadership?

PRAYER

Close the session with prayer.

Father, You've charged me with the calling of leadership. As a man under Your kingdom rule and authority, I accept that call in every area of my life, starting with own heart and will. Give me wisdom and insight to regularly and consistently live as the leader You've created me to be. In Christ's name, amen.

HIT THE STREETS
Overcoming Negative Outcomes

Negative outcomes always occur when a man sins. The Bible affirms this truth in harsh terms in Adam's story. Scripture calls the outcome death. Sin and death are always linked. You can't sin and not die. Every time sin is committed, a death also occurs—a separation somewhere in some form. This separation may be spiritual, emotional, or relational. James wrote:

> *When lust has conceived, it gives birth to sin; and*
> *when sin is accomplished, it brings forth death.*
> JAMES 1:15

You can overcome the negative outcomes of sin by applying the truth of God's Word to each form of death.

1. Spiritual Separation

A spiritual rift forms in your relationship with God when you sin. However, good news comes through the death, burial, and resurrection of Jesus Christ. Through Christ your relationship with God can be restored to a deep level of intimacy. But first you must confess your sins and repent:

> *If we confess our sins, He is faithful and righteous to forgive*
> *us our sins and to cleanse us from all unrighteousness.*
> 1 JOHN 1:9

2. Emotional Separation

One common negative outcome of sin is emotional death in your hopes, dreams, love, and self-worth. Over time the cumulative effect of emotional loss can lead to devastating results, whether through addictions, distancing yourself from other people, or simply shutting down. However, when you repent of our sins, God restores your emotional well-being:

> *After you have suffered for a little while, the God of all grace, who called you to His eternal glory in Christ, will Himself perfect, confirm, strengthen and establish you.*
> 1 PETER 5:10

3. Relational Separation

Difficulties in your relationships—in your family, your work, or your social circle—are a direct result of sin. Whether this separation occurs because of your own sins or those of others, forgiving yourself or the person who wronged you will usher in relational healing. Paul reminds us where to begin and, more important, why:

> *Be kind to one another, tender-hearted, forgiving each other, just as God in Christ also has forgiven you.*
> EPHESIANS 4:32

Sin brings about negative outcomes, but you can overcome them by applying these scriptural principles to the spiritual, emotional, and relational spheres of life.

BIBLE STUDY 1
Shame on You

Adam and Eve hid from God in the garden primarily because of their shame. When their eyes had been opened to their fallibility and sin, they sought to cover themselves with whatever they could find and then hid in the garden.

"Shame on you" is a common phrase parents may tell their children in an effort to correct behavior. Maybe a teacher said it to you when you were in elementary school. The phrase seeks to let someone know that his behavior doesn't align with the expectations of the authority figure. You may have also heard a statement that frequently follows: "You should have known better." That's often true. We probably did know better.

Read Genesis 2:25–3:12 and answer the following questions.

What happened between Genesis 2:25 and Genesis 3:10 that caused Adam to feel shame about his nakedness?

In what way does personal sin contribute to our feelings of shame and fear?

Shame causes many people to hide, not only from God but also from themselves and the people they love. Shame leaves its indelible imprint on your psyche at such a deep level that you may feel other people know what you did just by looking at you. It dampens your confidence, destroys your dignity, and silences your speech. Shame is a tool Satan employs to sideline the children of God. All true leadership is rooted in God's leadership, and shame keeps you from embracing His leadership and from drawing near "with confidence to the throne of grace" (Heb. 4:16).

Whom did God question first? How did Adam's sin cause him to exercise weak leadership?

How can personal shame disrupt intimacy in our relationships? Why does Satan seek to divide our relationships?

Eve ate the fruit when Adam wasn't watching. He wasn't exercising care over creation as God had commanded him. Notice that God asked Adam where he was, not Eve. This doesn't mean God didn't hold Eve accountable for her actions, but it seems to indicate that God held Adam to a standard of leadership that Adam hadn't met. Next Adam blamed both God and Eve because it was He who gave Eve to Adam and the fruit to Eve. Weak leadership is always born in sin and often breaks down our relationships.

Has shame ever created distance in your relationship with God? If so, in what ways?

In today's economy and virtual-connectivity workplace, many businesses are shifting to an off-site work arrangement. Fewer and fewer employees are required to put in a forty-hour workweek at the office. Texts, virtual meetings, and email allow us to communicate, but they don't allow the opportunity for a greater level of nonverbal feedback and intuitive understanding. Studies indicate that 93 percent of all our communication is nonverbal. Remove that element of proximity, and you remove much of the communication process altogether.

That's exactly why Satan sought to remove Adam and Eve from regular proximity with God. He knew if he could reduce the face-to-face time they shared with their Creator, he could significantly interfere with God's purposes and plans in and through their lives. Shame makes meaningful dialogue and intimate sharing a struggle rather than a flow.

NO MORE EXCUSES

What should Adam have done instead of running away from God?

Adam went in the opposite direction of God's presence when he experienced shame. And so do we. If Satan can keep us from walking with God in the cool of the day, he can keep much of what God wants to accomplish through us from being done as well.

Sin negatively affects our relationship with God at such a deep level that we can literally start to avoid Him and go into spiritual hiding. Somehow we convince ourselves that if we do, God won't know the things we've done, said, seen, or thought. Strong leadership means we take ownership over our sins and failings and don't allow sin to hinder our relationship with God.

Weak leadership shirks responsibility. Strong leadership humbly admits a mistake and receives forgiveness. How should we approach God when we've sinned?

Be honest with God. Be authentic. Come clean. Throw away the fig leaves. They'll wear out anyhow, and they don't look all that good on you. Shame is a tool of Satan to keep you from living out your full purpose and destiny. It's a clever tool that holds many men back. But if there were no such thing as sin, there would have been no need for a Savior. Jesus died so that your sin wouldn't enslave you. You're forgiven. You're clean. He paid the price. You don't have to hide and fail to accept responsibility.

Read the following verse.

There is now no condemnation for those who are in Christ Jesus.
ROMANS 8:1

Are you willing to let your shame go and accept Christ's complete forgiveness?

God knew where to find Adam, and He knows where to find you too. And when He does, He will have three questions for you similar to those He asked Adam:

1. "Where are you?" (Gen. 3:9).
2. "Who told you that you were naked?" (Gen. 3:11).
3. "What is this you have done?" (Gen. 3:13).

God is asking you these questions so that you can answer them, not because He doesn't know. He wants to see whether you're going to tell Him and yourself the truth. He doesn't want to hear you say you made a mistake or had a temporary lapse in judgment. It's deeper than that. Sinful rebellion against a holy God brings consequences. Repentance must come with an honest acknowledgment of what you've done.

All of the issues and crises we face today because of sin in the world have nothing to do with fruit. They have to do with what the fruit stood for, what it meant. Eating the fruit declared that Adam and Eve wanted to be like God. They wanted to be their own gods. The defining issue was whether they wanted to surrender to God or make their own decisions. Because they chose to exalt themselves above God's rule and reign in their lives, they broke fellowship with God. The natural outgrowth of their sin caused them to hide and separate themselves from the intimacy they once knew.

List some ways men seek to make their own decisions in our culture apart from God's leadership.

PRAY

Pray about your willingness to come clean with God. Ask Him to remove any residue of shame that may still linger in your life. Praise Him that in Christ you're fully forgiven and can access His authority and rule with all the boldness and courage that come from a relationship with Him.

It Just Keeps Going and Going and Going

You've probably heard of the Energizer Bunny. This pink toy has spent decades advertising the power of the Energizer brand of batteries. The message is that if you use Energizer batteries, the devices in which they're placed will have enough power to last longer than you can imagine. They'll just keep going and going and going. It's a cute and sometimes annoying ad, but it definitely gets its point across.

Men, your impact as a leader will keep going and going and going as well. Whether that impact is good or bad, the repercussions will last longer than you might imagine, especially in your family. In Exodus God tells us that the consequences we earn through wrong choices will be generationally passed down through our seed:

> *You shall not worship [idols] or serve them; for I, the LORD your God, am a jealous God, visiting the iniquity of the fathers on the children, on the third and the fourth generations of those who hate Me, but showing lovingkindness to thousands, to those who love Me and keep My commandments.*
> EXODUS 20:5-6

Notice that God also said He will give blessings to thousands as well. What you do reaches far beyond just you:

- Children
- Grandchildren
- Workmates
- Business partners
- Community
- Church

That's just to name a few of the people you influence. It's a sobering thought, isn't it? It wouldn't be so bad if my mistakes were left with me. But my mistakes are passed on and on to many succeeding generations. They also affect people where I work, the church where I worship, and my neighborhood and community.

Of course, the principle works the other way too. My faithfulness can bless my family and my sphere of influence for generations. It's no wonder Satan targets men. He understands this legacy relationship. He knows the damage he can do if he can produce legacies of destruction rather than greatness.

Read the following verse.

> *One generation shall praise Your works to another,*
> *And shall declare Your mighty acts.*
> PSALM 145:4

What must happen first in our hearts for us to declare God's mighty acts to the next generation?

What unique responsibility do men bear to transmit faith to the next generation? What does that responsibility look like in practice?

We must be men in whom and through whom God can perform mighty acts in order for these to be passed down to future generations. Becoming that kind of man starts with our usefulness to God as leaders. Have you ever met a man who's still talking about what God did thirty or forty years ago, as if that's the most current work God has done in his life? If you have to reach that far back to recount a great work of God, you might need to reexamine your relationship with Him. God is in the business of working regularly.

NO MORE EXCUSES

Why is it important for younger generations to hear and witness God's mighty work being done in and through an older generation that isn't merely resting on God's past faithfulness?

A Fox News article once listed reasons millennials are turning away from God and the church. Among the most prominent reasons is the lack of authenticity among adults who are older than they. In other words, young adults aren't seeing God's mighty acts modeled or hearing them proclaimed.[1]

When was the most recent time you either described or modeled God's mighty work in your life for someone younger than you?

Why is it important to demonstrate an authentic relationship with God to the people we lead?

To our forefathers, faith was an experience. To our fathers, faith was an inheritance. To us, faith is a convenience. To the next generation, faith is a nuisance. Why? Because men have failed to model faith as the living, abiding, powerful relationship with God it's meant to be. We've failed to demonstrate any genuine level of discipline or commitment.

A disciplined commitment to faith means sticking to it and avoiding diversions that will distract you from making a kingdom impact at home, in your church, and in your community. George Allen was the coach of the Washington Redskins in the early 1970s. He was invited to the White House for a dinner, but the dinner was scheduled for the last week of January. Allen turned down the president's invitation because he was preparing his team for the Super Bowl, and he didn't want anything to distract him from his task, even if it was the president. Allen had no objection to dining at the White House, but the timing would have undermined his priorities.

What are some actions a man can take to guide those he leads to a greater level of faith?

Describe the difference in importance between talking about your faith and modeling a life of faith for those you lead.

As I enter the later decades of my life, this concept of legacy seems to crop up more than it used to. I find myself thinking about what matters most. What am I leaving behind? What impact can I still make even after I'm no longer here? How can I continue to contribute to kingdom growth, not only in my family but also in other areas of influence?

Men, it's never too early to examine your leadership strategies and incorporate legacy thinking into all of them. Invest in what will last for eternity. Spend your time strengthening others in the faith. A legacy of faith lasts throughout eternity.

PRAY

Pray that God will reveal to you more areas of impact than you're currently aware of. Ask Him to show you ways you can begin investing in a legacy as a kingdom man. Pray about ways you're influencing your family. Ask God to give you grace to lead and love even better in your home and in your extended family.

1. Alex McFarland, "Ten Reasons Millennials Are Backing Away from God and Christianity," Fox News, April 30, 2017, https://www.foxnews.com/opinion/ten-reasons-millennials-are-backing-away-from-god-and-christianity.

Week 4
NO MORE GOING THROUGH THE MOTIONS

START

Welcome to group session 4 of No More Excuses.

Last week we considered an issue that's all too common among men: weak leadership.

Weak leadership has effects that extend beyond us. What's one area in which you've been convicted to lead?

No boxing champion attained that status by simply going through the motions. No Olympic gold medalist reached that pinnacle of achievement through a ho-hum attitude of routine. Settling into predictability gets a man stuck in a dangerous location: the comfort zone. Nothing amazing ever came from a comfort zone.

Describe common results associated with going through the motions.

In what ways does going through the motions contribute to a life of mediocrity?

Meaning is found beyond merely going through the motions. It comes when you commit to a sold-out, all-in, no-turning-back pursuit of God Himself. He's ready. Are you? Let's look together at Solomon's quest for meaning and learn how it relates to men today.

Ask someone to pray before watching the video teaching.

WATCH

SESSION 4 Video. *To access the teaching sessions,*
use the instructions in the back of your Bible study book.

Far too many men are living without substance in their lives.

When a man disconnects from God, he's disconnected from the source of meaning.

If all of life is only in this life, you'll never have the life that you're looking for.
You'll just go through the motions.

Only when a man brings forever into time, only when heaven is integrated into history
is meaning brought to the activities.

God will allow meaninglessness in the life of a man who does things without Him
being connected to it.

God says, "In this world you leave Me out, and you are not going to be able to break
out and to experience life as I intended it to be experienced."

Make God your priority, and He will inject meaning in your life because He will make
eternity enter time.

God says, "When I don't define who you are as a man and you let any and everything
else define your manhood, your manhood is in trouble because your manhood will
be without meaning."

MAN UP

Use the following questions to discuss the video teaching.

Read the following verse together.

*The conclusion, when all has been heard, is: fear God and
keep His commandments, because this applies to every person.*
ECCLESIASTES 12:13

Solomon had it all. Status. Power. Fame. Money. Women. Freedom. Attention. Control.
You name it; he had it. You'd think he would have been the happiest man on earth, but he
wasn't. In fact, the man who had it all spent an inordinate amount of his time pondering
the meaning of life. He couldn't quite figure out why he was here and what he should do.

Neither Solomon's pursuits nor his conquests gave him the kind of satisfaction that lasts
longer than a good meal or a movie. He wanted more. He wanted authentic meaning, the
kind that doesn't depend on other people's validation, a paycheck, or a contest to win.

**In what ways does Solomon's pursuit of significance and meaning mirror
many men's quests today?**

**How can a lack of meaning contribute to a lifestyle of resignation just
to go through the motions?**

Going through the motions creates a life that looks like life but without the meaning.
It takes our responsibilities at work, to our families, to God, and to others and makes them
nothing more than a routine. It saps all meaning and purpose from our lives.

Because we've been created in the image of God, we have an inherent need for meaning,
creativity, significance, and purpose. We mirror God's greatness within us, so a life in
which we merely go through the motions is wearisome for us, not only physically but also
emotionally, spiritually, and psychologically.

**Brainstorm some creative ways to break out of the box of going through
the motions. Begin with your spiritual life. Then move outward.**

On the video Dr. Evans said, "We have men today who are busy doing stuff like building careers, making money, playing sports, and more, but they are asking or desiring the thing they are doing to give them the meaning in doing it. And that's what God will not allow." Meaning can't be found apart from God because God is the Source of all meaning.

What are some common places men look for meaning other than God?

Read James 4:13-16. God supplies meaning in your life because He supplies life itself. Nothing exists outside His direct supply. The primary principle in identifying your purpose and, as a result, identifying your meaning involves locating God. Don't search for yourself, your purpose, or your significance. Search for God. He knows where those goals lie.

Have you seen someone make plans, only to have God intervene and suddenly change those plans? What did they learn?

Solomon arrived at this conclusion when all was said and done: "Fear God and keep His commandments" (Eccl. 12:13). I like to say it this way: align your thoughts, words, and actions underneath the overarching rule of God in every area of your life. That's God's kingdom agenda for you. When you do that, you'll experience the visible manifestation of His power and purpose both in and through you.

Identify one specific way you can align your thoughts, words, or actions this week underneath God's overarching rule.

PRAYER
Close the session with prayer.

Father, mold us into men of meaning and significance. Give us wisdom to avoid spending our lives in futility and instead to pursue You and Your purposes. Help us break out of our comfort zones of going through the motions and discover lives of significance as You work in and through us. In Christ's name, amen.

HIT THE STREETS

Three Steps to Success

If you want to find the secret to life and success, look to the Author of life. In other words, if you want to find your purpose, don't go looking for your purpose. Look for the Purpose Giver. The clearest way to find out who you are isn't to look at the man in the mirror but to look at God, the One who gives you your identity. When you find your Creator, you find you. God has given us three clear steps we can follow to live a life of success.

1. Fear God

To fear God doesn't mean the kind of fear you might get if you watch a thriller or get lost in a strange city late at night. Fear of God involves reverence and honor. It's similar to the fear you'd give a judge in a courtroom or a high-ranking government official. Fearing God shows up in your thoughts and actions when God influences them. When you seek to align what you do and who you are with Him and His revealed will, you're living a life that fears God.

2. Keep His Commandments

God has revealed a number of commandments throughout Scripture, but if you want a sure way of knowing how to obey them all, He has given us two to summarize. Jesus said you must love God and love others:

> *You shall love the Lord your God with all your heart, and with all your soul, and with all your mind. You shall love your neighbor as yourself.*
> MATTHEW 22:37,39

When you obey these two commandments completely, you'll naturally live out all of the other commandments. Love is compassionately and righteously pursuing the well-being of another person. It isn't first and foremost an emotion. Love is an action. Make loving God and loving others your highest commitment in life, and you'll be a spiritual success in all you do.

3. Include God in Your Planning

Planning is good and important, but excluding God from your planning is a sure way to head in the wrong direction. James boldly tells us:

> *Come now, you who say, "Today or tomorrow we will go*
> *to such and such a city, and spend a year there and engage*
> *in business and make a profit." Yet you do not know what your*
> *life will be like tomorrow. You are just a vapor that appears*
> *for a little while and then vanishes away. Instead, you ought*
> *to say, "If the Lord wills, we will live and also do this or that."*
> *But as it is, you boast in your arrogance; all such boasting is evil.*
> JAMES 4:13-16

Including God in your planning means bringing His perspective to bear on all you do. It also leaves room for the Holy Spirit to shift your thinking and your plans midstream.

Fearing God, keeping His commandments, and including God in your planning are three critical components for living out the full expression of the man God designed you to be. God created you to be great and to fulfill your destiny. By following His road map, you'll discover a life of purpose and fulfillment you never dreamed possible.

BIBLE STUDY 1
Chasing the Wind

I was on a cruise a couple of years ago, and as I stood on the boat looking out over the vast ocean, I recognized my insignificance. All around me was water, the largest body of water in the world. Here I was, a little speck on a boat that seemed huge to me but that was itself a tiny speck in the middle of that huge ocean.

When I turned around and looked at the stern of the boat, I noticed a striking phenomenon. As the ship sailed through the water, it caused a lot of turbulence and created a dent in the water. A couple of seconds later, however, the water closed the gap, and everything was back to normal. The ship had left no permanent mark on the ocean.

What impact do you hope to have had on the world when your time here is done?

What steps are you taking to ensure that's the legacy you're leaving?

Legacy is an important subject on my mind right now, as it should be on the mind of every man. Too many of us go through our lives and leave little or no impact for good. Even King Solomon wrestled with this fear. Having a purpose and leaving an impact for God's kingdom matter. But how do we do that according to God's kingdom plan?

Read Ecclesiastes 1:12-15 and answer the following questions.

What's the "grievous task" (v. 13) Solomon referred to in this passage?

Describe the result of "striving after wind" (v. 14). How does this illustration apply to a life lived outside God's prescribed plan?

Do you ever struggle with your own meaning or purpose? If so, how does that struggle affect your emotions or productivity?

What does chasing the wind look like in your life? How closely is the struggle for meaning and purpose tied to chasing the wind?

If you've ever tried to catch wind, you know it's uncatchable. Not only are we blind to its movement, but we also can't touch it. It's impossible to catch something you can't see or touch. Yet that's exactly what King Solomon compared life on earth to. Life lived apart from God's divine wisdom and plan amounts to nothing more than the futile pursuit of "striving after wind" (v. 14).

We start to chase the wind when we go through life without giving thought to our eternal purpose or to God's leadership in our lives. When that happens, other goals replace the goal of knowing and living for Him, and we chase a life that truly isn't worth having.

List some benefits King Solomon must have experienced in his life, whether they're in the area of pleasure, finances, work, or power.

Despite having these benefits, King Solomon said his life was meaningless ("vanity," v. 14) apart from God's rule and authority Why do you think God's rule and authority play such a critical role in our own pursuit of significance and satisfaction?

NO MORE EXCUSES

God has put within each one of us a sense of the eternal, a yearning for things beyond space and time, desires like ultimate purpose and meaning. Although God has set us in the mundane routine of earthly life, He wants us to look beyond the realm of earth for something greater.

> **Read Ecclesiastes 3:11. When have you felt the pull of eternity in your soul? How might this longing motivate us to live a life that goes beyond merely checking off tasks and going through the motions?**

You can't find your ultimate purpose in life by looking at life on this earth. The only way you can find the answer to the eternal question of purpose, significance, and meaning that echoes loudly in your heart is by looking into eternity's definition of these ideals. And when you looks into eternity's perspective, you'll find God's answer waiting for you.

The minute you start looking at life to find the meaning of life, you miss the very life you're looking for. As long as you focus on wealth, power, pleasure, work, people, or anything else to find the meaning of life, you've lost what you're looking for.

> **What are some common pursuits that men use today to define their significance or meaning?**

> **Why is it important to focus only on God and His view of your significance and meaning?**

Men often find their significance and meaning in their careers or in their roles as a husband and provider. Although these are good gifts from a God who loves us, if we don't pursue those purposes with God's eternal purpose in mind, we're simply going through the motions. We'll fall short of the glory that God has given us. Our wheels are turning, but we aren't getting anywhere.

Only when you view life as God's gift can you begin to find its purpose. Only when you live in time from the perspective of eternity can you find life's meaning. In other words, if you want to find your purpose, don't go looking for your purpose. Look for the Purpose Giver. If you want to find the secret to life, look to the Author of life. When you find your Creator, you find you.

Jesus said:

> *I came that they may have life, and have it abundantly.*
> JOHN 10:10

Life isn't found in the living but in the Living One. Jesus agreed with Solomon. Life is a gift from God, and He defines it for you.

In what ways are you merely going through the motions?

God often uses our past experiences, as well as our gifts, passions, and opportunities, to lead us to our ultimate purpose in Him. Consider those aspects of your life. How could you continue to pursue these same passions in ways that bring ultimate honor and glory to God?

PRAY

Pray about aligning all of your life underneath God's overarching, comprehensive rule. Ask God to reveal more answers to the previous questions and to fine-tune your understanding of His purpose for you. Seek to obey Him by reading, meditating on, and studying His Word. Praise Him for the purpose He created you to fulfill.

BIBLE STUDY 2
Get to Work

My doctor uses every opportunity he can to present the gospel. In the physical-health world he's pretty famous, being credited as the founder of aerobic exercise. Dr. Cooper has always believed in pursuing great health. "But Tony," he tells me when I go in for my regular checkup, "this is just a platform I use to introduce people to God." Dr. Cooper has found his calling in his work. Many people do. Maybe you do your work to fulfill your responsibility to your family and to pay your bills without having a sense of personal calling to your career. You can still do more than simply go through the motions when you dedicate your work to the Lord.

Solomon tells us that finding satisfaction in our work is a gift from God Himself. And Paul reminds us that whatever work we do, we're to work for God, knowing He's our ultimate boss.

Read the following verses.

> *There is nothing better for a man than to eat and drink and tell himself that his labor is good. This also I have seen that it is from the hand of God.*
> ECCLESIASTES 2:24

> *Whatever you do, do your work heartily, as for the Lord rather than for men, knowing that from the Lord you will receive the reward of the inheritance. It is the Lord Christ whom you serve.*
> COLOSSIANS 3:23-24

How can knowing that work is a gift from God and that God is the One you serve help you escape the rut of going through the motions in your job?

Describe the difference between going through the motions at work and fully engaging in the job.

God can give you the ability to enjoy your labor. That process starts with your relationship with Him, but it should extend to the environment where you expend your labor. God wants you to have a job you enjoy doing and can do well for His glory.

There's nothing worse than having to get up and go to a job you hate. But do you know why a lot of men feel that way about their work? Because they're laying bricks instead of building cathedrals. It's a problem of perspective.

The goal of work isn't to put in your forty hours a week for forty years so that you can retire. Nor is the goal the accumulation of wealth so that you don't have to work anymore. The goal of work is to make a lasting impact for God. That's God's goal, so that should be your goal.

What are some ways you can do your job so that God receives the ultimate glory for your work? Do you know anyone who does this well?

Once a close family member had to undergo surgery, and her family gathered at the hospital prior to the procedure. When the doctors and nurses came in to consult with her about the surgery, they did more than that. They called all of the family members around and made it clear they do their work for the Lord. Though the knife would be in the surgeon's hand, it was God who guided. Though medication could provide healing or prevent infection, it was God who granted these results. Then they openly prayed with everyone, inviting God into the surgery room so that His presence and wisdom would dominate.

Each of us can see our jobs with an eternal perspective. The person in the cubicle next to us isn't just a coworker but someone made in the image of God with an eternal soul. If they don't know Jesus, we have the opportunity to introduce our coworker to Him through our words and actions. Beyond that, we can serve one another sacrificially by lending a hand or offering an encouraging word. When we start to believe God placed us in our jobs, it changes our perspective.

NO MORE EXCUSES

How does our fear of what people think or what they might say keep us from boldly proclaiming God's name in the workplace?

When you understand that God alone is your Source and that everyone and everything else is a resource, you won't give in to fear and remain quiet about His name. Most men spend the bulk of their time in the workplace. Serving and working well are great, but never leaving a lasting impact for the Lord Jesus Christ would be a waste of that time.

Why is it important to understand that God is your Source?

In what ways does knowing that spiritual truth free you to do all God has called you to do?

Living as a testimony to Christ in the workplace doesn't always have to be passing out tracts or giving a verbal witness. You can model integrity and set yourself apart as Daniel did when he lived and worked in the pagan kingdom of Babylon.

Super Bowl-winning coach Tony Dungy, a friend of mine, had the rare opportunity to play on what's arguably the best defense in the NFL during the height of its dominance—the Pittsburgh Steelers in the 1970s. The Steel Curtain, as it was known, could crush opponents with just a stare. They were that great. But Dungy recently shared one of the secrets of the team's success.

He said most people thought the Steelers' defensive players were great because they were so committed to football and to winning. Although they were, Dungy revealed that they had a commitment even higher than that. They were committed to working for the Lord. To them, playing football was their job. Winning games was their job. This strong work ethic showed up in all they did because they believed and publicly proclaimed in the locker room that to give all their effort was the way to serve God. God expected nothing less than their best.

Dungy said most of the players showed up early for practice and stayed late, and they encouraged others to do the same. The reward of their work resulted in (at the time of this writing) a franchise with the most Super Bowl wins in the history of football. Their eternal rewards will be awaiting them as well.

Working hard and being all you can be are part of God's design for you. God Himself worked in establishing His creation and maintaining it. Similarly, Jesus spent His whole earthly life working. We can assume He worked hard in Joseph's carpenter shop, and He spent His entire ministry working out the will of His Father. On the cross He stated that His work was finished (see John 19:30).

Men, simply going through the motions in life and at work wastes your God-given opportunities to do your job in a way that brings God all the glory. Because you're working for God and not for yourself, you have good reason to work hard and to the best of your ability. Whatever you're doing, big or small, do it with all your heart as to the Lord (see Eph. 6:7). He will see your work, and He will reward you.

Read Ephesians 6:7. What changes about your job when you see the Lord as your ultimate boss?

What's one concrete step you can take to be more fully engaged at work in the hopes that your coworkers will see your good work and give glory to your Father in heaven?

PRAY

Pray and commit your work to the Lord. Proverbs 16:3 says if you commit your work to the Lord, "your plans will be established." Every day when you wake up, say a prayer asking God to use you on the job or in your career and workplace for His kingdom purposes.

Week 5
NO MORE COMPROMISING YOUR INTEGRITY

START

Welcome to group session 5 of No More Excuses.

Last week we examined the dangers of going through the motions. Why is going through the motions such an easy pattern to fall into if we're not diligent?

True integrity defines who we are when no one can see us. It involves words we say and actions we do in private or with a limited number of people present. Words said behind closed doors or in a locker room often reveal who we really are far more clearly than our public persona.

What actions come to mind when you hear that a man has compromised his integrity?

Why is maintaining your integrity so important?

We may think we can hide who we really are in secret, but God sees. God knows. And often in His providential ways, other people come to know as well. Just ask more than twenty high-profile business leaders, celebrities, and talk-show hosts who lost their jobs in the past few years over something they said in private. In contrast, true integrity doesn't shift based on the people present or on the location. True integrity stays consistent throughout each moment of our lives.

Ask someone to pray before watching the video teaching.

WATCH

Far too many men are signaling one way while living another.

Integrity: living up to one's legitimate standards

It is when men decide that God will set the standard and it is that standard they will pursue that we become men of integrity, and we have the impact this society, our families, and we ourselves so desperately need.

We've allowed the world to dumb down God's standard of manhood, what it means to be a husband and a father, our roles in the church, and the influence we are to be making on society.

We want God to show up with our lack of integrity, but God shows up when we demonstrate integrity.

If you don't have that kind of faith in God, you'll compromise your integrity because you think men make the final decision, that people are the final arbiters of your well-being, that people are the source of your career.

Sometimes when you maintain integrity as a man, it will cost you.

You will find yourself, as a man, in the lions' den, and God expects you to keep the standard.

God can give you back the integrity you think you lost.

MAN UP

Use the following questions to discuss the video teaching.

Read the following verse together.

*Now when Daniel knew that the document was signed,
he entered his house (now in his roof chamber he had
windows open toward Jerusalem); and he continued
kneeling on his knees three times a day, praying and giving
thanks before his God, as he had been doing previously.*
DANIEL 6:10

As a child, you probably heard the story of Daniel in the lion's den, or as a parent, you may have told it to your children. We often focus on the lions and their refusal to eat Daniel for dinner. Yet an important principle in this story is often overshadowed by the sensational aspect of God's power over lions—the principle of Daniel's consistent integrity.

Why did Daniel leave his windows open when he prayed rather than rationalizing that he should protect himself by closing them?

Describe some ways men may seek to rationalize our way out of complete obedience to God in the face of risk.

A particular group of African animals is known as the big five—the largest, most well-known animals in Africa. Though these big animals are fun to see, the continent also has a large number of other animals that are just as much fun to see. The idea of compromising a person's integrity is often applied to certain big sins as well, while the myriad ways most men compromise their integrity are ignored. We might classify sins like adultery, fraud, embezzlement, drugs, and pornography as the big five. In reality, from God's perspective, if Daniel had chosen not to pray, he would have seriously compromised his integrity.

What are some ways men might compromise their integrity in God's eyes?

On the video Dr. Evans said, "What far too many of us as men are doing is we're lowering the standard—dunking at a lower standard and thinking we've done something. Rather than keeping God's standard high and saying we've got to raise ourselves to meet His standard, we've allowed the world to dumb down God's standard of manhood and to dumb down God's standard of what it means to be a husband and a father and to dumb down God's standard of our roles in the church and to dumb down the influence we're to be having. We ought to be making an impact on society. Therefore, we have dumbed down our integrity."

Identify ways we've dumbed down God's standard of biblical manhood and, as a result, are failing to make an impact on society.

Daniel could pray with the window open because he believed God was his Source. God owned the outcome. Men, God is your Source. Your boss isn't your source. Your health isn't. Even your family isn't. Although we may have a say, no one has the final say but God.

How can believing God is your Source free you to make decisions rooted in biblical integrity?

God has a standard of integrity. It isn't hidden from us but disclosed in His Word. We're all called to love God and demonstrate His love to others. This is the basis of all ethical living in God's kingdom. His standard encompasses all of life. If you haven't lived up to this standard in the past, you can start today. Start now. Never let fear dictate your decisions. God has your back when you align your life under His standard.

What's one practical action you can take this week to align yourself more fully with God's standard of biblical manhood? It could be something you do at work, at home, or in your personal spiritual development. Commit to hold one another accountable at the next group session.

PRAYER

Close the session with prayer.

Father, in a culture that consistently lowers standards, we want
to remain focused on You. We want to aim high in all we do, knowing
we serve an audience of one. Convict us when our integrity needs
to improve. Forgive us when we've failed You in the past. Strengthen
us to live according to Your standard. In Christ's name, amen.

HIT THE STREETS

How to Internalize Integrity

Living a life of integrity includes all areas of your life. Your public integrity is what other people see in the workplace or in your home and church. Your private integrity exists between you and God, applying to what you say and do when no one else will find out. Keeping your integrity level high is God's standard for you as a man. Blessings will come as a result of your personal integrity, just as Daniel experienced protection from the lions when thrown into their den.

Here are five ways a kingdom man can cultivate integrity.

1. Don't Wait Around

Don't wait for your boss, your wife, or your environment to improve before you make a move. Integrity refers to who you are on the inside, regardless of what's happening on the outside. Don't blame others if your level of integrity isn't what it should be.

2. Set Your Standards in Advance

Decide on the standards you won't compromise before you find yourself in the middle of a problem. You can't become a man of integrity on the spot. You can't wait until the action gets hot and heavy to make decisions of integrity. Establish biblical guidelines for integrity in advance.

3. Develop a Regular Devotional Life

Make spending time with God the rule, not the exception. As you see in Daniel's case, cultivating your walk with God throughout the day will do more than anything else to help you become a man of integrity.

4. Find Friends Who Will Hold You Accountable

Find friends who ask hard questions about what you're doing and not doing. Be authentic. Cultivate trust in the relationship that allows you to share failures. Don't judge, and you won't be judged (see Luke 6:37). Stay in contact and reach out when you need a reminder to stay strong.

5. Major on God, Not Your Circumstances

If Daniel had majored on his circumstances, he would never have maintained his integrity. He would have compromised just like everybody else. He would no longer have been an extraordinary man who was living for God's purposes. God didn't save you so that you could become like everybody else. He saved you to be extraordinary.

BIBLE STUDY 1
Walk Securely

Integrity is a critical issue today. In a society where people feel they can't trust anyone anymore, integrity is a very important subject. It's important for the business owner who's looking for employees he can trust. It's critical for the church that's looking for godly leaders they can follow. And it's vital for a generation of young men who need role models who'll lead them into lives of purpose, meaning, and impact.

When we talk about integrity, we're talking about a person's trustworthiness. The word *integrity* means "complete" or "whole." It means what you say and what you mean are the same thing. It means when you make a promise, you keep it. It means when you say you'll do something, you do it.

Read the following verse and answer the questions.

He who walks in integrity walks securely,
But he who perverts his ways will be found out.
PROVERBS 10:9

What does it mean to live with integrity?

This verse says a lack of integrity "will be found out." Do you believe this? Other than public exposure, how will a lack of integrity be found out?

What does it mean to walk securely?

How can knowing you walk securely contribute to your peace of mind?

There are two ways to live—with or without integrity. Our folly always has a way of being revealed. Even if others don't realize our lack of integrity, God does. Nothing is hidden from His sight (see Heb. 4:13). What's more, God sees beyond the surface and into a man's heart. His sight goes beyond our conduct and into our character and motivation. God always knows our lack of integrity. In contrast, men who've trusted Christ and are committed to living in line with His standard walk securely, knowing they're right with God and others.

What are some ways Satan seeks to trap us so that we'll compromise our integrity?

Most men have compromised their integrity at some point. It may have been at a newsstand or at the gift shop at the airport, when you looked around and made sure no one was watching before you picked up a magazine. Or maybe you've turned your phone, computer, or iPad to private-browsing mode and hit the porn sites. After all, who would ever know?

Compromise may not involve anything you're doing. It may all be in your mind. Nonetheless, compromise is still at play because integrity has to do with more than your outward behavior. Integrity is about more than conduct; it's about what happens in your heart.

Would you describe yourself as a person of integrity? Would your friends and family agree?

When we talk about integrity, we aren't talking about your reputation. Your reputation is what other people think of you. Integrity goes beyond that to what you're really like on the inside. It refers to your character.

NO MORE EXCUSES

What you do when no one is watching is who you are. What you do in secret and what you may think you got away with will come out in God's economy because the spiritual principle in Proverbs 10:9 holds true. That's why honesty and repentance are key. Only those qualities can prevent the consequences of compromising your integrity.

The word *repentance* means to make a 180-degree turn. It means turning from your sin and trusting in Christ. Why is it important to accept God's forgiveness, mercy, and grace when you've failed?

Why are we often reluctant to do this?

Jesus' atonement covers all sins at all levels in all ways. Accepting His forgiveness, however, can sometimes be more difficult for some sins than others. Why? Mostly because our culture puts a higher emphasis on some sins than others. As a result, far too many men fall back into sin because they live under the chains and oppression of unconfessed sin or unreceived forgiveness.

If we're going to be men of integrity rather than look for an excuse to take the easy way out, it will boil down to our personal walk with God. It will come down to our ability to trust Christ's forgiveness of all our sins and to walk in the newness of His love. When we're right with God, we're then able to treat others the way He has called us to do.

Read Psalm 119:9-16. What help has God given us to live according to His standard?

Identify concrete wisdom in this passage for maintaining integrity.

We'll live with integrity only to the degree that we meet God's standard. God hasn't left us on our own. He cares about our integrity and has given us His Word so that we understand what it means to live in a relationship with Him. The more we focus on His Word, hide it in our hearts, and model our lives after the wisdom we find there, the more we'll be men of integrity. But even in moments when we're pressed to make a choice that doesn't honor God, He has given us help:

No temptation has overtaken you but such as is common
to man; and God is faithful, who will not allow
you to be tempted beyond what you are able, but
with the temptation will provide the way of escape
also, so that you will be able to endure it.
1 CORINTHIANS 10:13

When we're tempted, God knows. Thankfully, He has given us a way out. If you know Jesus, He's alive and working in your life. You don't have to succumb to temptation or compromise your integrity. He's present with you to help you overcome.

When you're tempted, why is it helpful to realize that you have a way out?

The next time you're tempted to compromise your integrity, how will you respond?

PRAY

Ask God to reveal areas in which you may not recognize a lapse in your integrity so that you can identify it, repent of it, and live without compromise. Ask Him to show you ways you can encourage other men to live with integrity. Seek God's forgiveness for hurting anyone as a result of a lapse in your personal integrity.

BIBLE STUDY 2
Staying Strong in Difficulties

A man's integrity is severely tested in adversity. You know that as well as I do. If you hit your thumb with a hammer, that occasion lends itself to doing or saying something you shouldn't far more than if you're sitting in your easy chair drinking sweet tea. Difficulties diminish our resolve and kick-start our human nature to seek a way to cope.

If you want to know the level of your integrity, measure it at a time when circumstances aren't going well. What you're really like can be measured only when your life is falling apart.

Select the terms that best define you when life is toughest.

☐ **Patient**

☐ **Irritable**

☐ **Gracious**

☐ **Judgmental**

☐ **Trusting**

☐ **Fearful**

☐ **Affirming**

☐ **Destructive**

Kingdom men must be defined by the fruit of the Spirit, even when life is tough. Otherwise, we aren't living as men of integrity. In sports there are gracious losers and immature losers. Gracious losers know they can't win every game, and they congratulate the other team for a hard-fought battle. Immature losers internalize the difficulty, blame others, and often fail to grow as a result of the loss. Losses can send them spiraling downward in their personal lives as well as in their careers.

The fruit of the Spirit reveals the true level of your integrity, especially in the midst of life's toughest losses.

Read the following verses.

> *The fruit of the Spirit is love, joy, peace, patience, kindness, goodness, faithfulness, gentleness, self-control; against such things there is no law. Now those who belong to Christ Jesus have crucified the flesh with its passions and desires. If we live by the Spirit, let us also walk by the Spirit. Let us not become boastful, challenging one another, envying one another.*
> GALATIANS 5:22-26

Would you say these traits are evident in your life? How would greater dependence on Christ cultivate any that are lacking?

The fruit of the Spirit are supernatural attributes that followers of Jesus possess as they know Jesus and walk in the Holy Spirit. The word *fruit* in verse 22 is singular, both in English and in the original Greek language. In practical terms this means every Christian has all nine of these traits by virtue of being filled with the Holy Spirit. Although all Christians have at least one spiritual gift and individual Christians have different gifts or different blends of gifts, every Christian should be marked by love, joy, peace, patience, kindness, goodness, faithfulness, gentleness, and self-control. We may not possess all traits in equal measure, and they may be more evident to a greater degree in another man's life. But if you know Jesus, these traits are yours. Walking in the Spirit keeps us from indulging in sinful, integrity-stripping behaviors like boastfulness and envy.

What confidence does it give you to know these traits are yours simply by knowing Jesus?

NO MORE EXCUSES

How does walking with the Spirit and living in Him help you maintain your integrity?

Walking by the Spirit means we embrace the Holy Spirit's leading and work in our lives. It means we trust His guidance above our own. Yet even men who walk with the Spirit daily sometimes compromise. Maybe it's recently happened to you. Maybe it's going on right now.

You may be thinking as we study integrity, *I've already compromised. My wife doesn't trust me. My kids don't respect me. My boss knows I'm not dependable at work. It's too late for me.*

No, it's not. It's never too late with God. Think about men depicted in Scripture. Moses definitely lost his integrity when he killed the Egyptian, but God gave it back to him at a burning bush and called him to lead Israel. David lost his integrity with Bathsheba, but he confessed his sin, and God restored him. In fact, God regarded him as "a man after His own heart" (1 Sam. 13:14). These men had their faults, but they also trusted God and exercised genuine sorrow and repented for what they had done. They left their sin behind and embraced God's will for their life. You can too.

If you've recently compromised your integrity, with whom do you need to make amends after you've sought God's forgiveness?

What can we learn by seeing ways God used fallen and flawed men like Moses and David for His glory even after they sinned?

God is in the restoration business. He can take failure and turn it into a future of hope. He can take a mess and make a miracle. He can take compromise and restore it to commitment. But He won't do it alone. It requires cooperation on your part, a willingness to be restored to a life of integrity. Just as a person who restores furniture often has to strip the furniture to its original base before building it back up again, God sometimes strips us to our core before refinishing us with the shine of success.

Read the following verse.

> *Better is the poor who walks in his integrity*
> *Than he who is crooked though he be rich.*
> PROVERBS 28:6

Why is integrity foundational for us if we want to live as kingdom men? Do you pay as much attention to your integrity as you do to your success?

Over the next week review the fruit of the Spirit found in Galatians 5:22-23 and ask God daily to produce the fruit in your life. What practical effect do you imagine that exercise will have on your integrity?

Integrity isn't a subject that gets much airplay in our contemporary Christian circles. For whatever reason, preachers shy away from preaching on it, authors don't write about it, and small groups seek other subjects. But integrity stands as the foundation of our greatness as men. Until we return to embracing, encouraging, and fostering a spirit of integrity in ourselves and in others, we'll continue to face the fallout of ongoing compromise. As a result, we'll continue to fail in our pursuit to leave a lasting impact on and legacy for those around us. Let's be men with no more excuses. Let's live in the full realization of all God has created us to be.

PRAY

Pray that God will show you how to be more authentic
with other men and will foster integrity in your life and
relationships. Ask God to give you wisdom to lead in this
revolutionary cultural change, starting right where you are.

Week 6
NO MORE SIFTING THROUGH THE RUBBLE

START

Welcome to group session 6 of No More Excuses.

Over the past week you came to understand why the world needs men of integrity. I hope study this topic has increased your desire to be such a man. Let's share what we've learned.

Who's a man who models well what it means to live with integrity?
What's one lesson you can put into practice from his life?

This week we'll focus on sifting through the rubble—our response to failure. Michael Jordan once said, "I've missed more than nine thousand shots in my career. I've lost almost three hundred games. Twenty six times I've been trusted to take the game-winning shot and missed. I've failed over and over and over again in my life. And that is why I succeed."[1] Thomas Edison said, "I have not failed; I've just found ten thousand ways that won't work."[2]

What are some common responses to failure (examples: blaming others and feeling shame)?

In what ways can failure contribute to greater success in the future?

Our failures, when responded to with the right mindset, can propel us into greater levels of spiritual development and achievement. But far too often men allow their failures to define, confine, and resign them to lives of mediocrity. The fear of failure is one of the greatest deterrents to risk and faith. But God has something to say about facing our failures head-on, and He shares it with us over breakfast.

Ask someone to pray before watching the video teaching.

1. Michael Jordan, BrainyQuote, accessed February 25, 2019, https://www.brainyquote.com/quotes/michael_jordan_127660.
2. Thomas Edison, ibid., https://www.brainyquote.com/quotes/thomas_a_edison_132683.

WATCH

SESSION 6 Video. *To access the teaching sessions,*
use the instructions in the back of your Bible study book.

We are dependent on God, and we are never to be independent from Him.

God offers that opportunity of grace to every man who's willing to recognize their failure, acknowledge their failure, repent of their failure, and return to the One they failed.

God will give you as many chances as you are willing to take advantage of.

God wants to build something new in your life on the space of your failure.

A lot of men are praying, "God, do something with me, change me, rebuild me, reuse me" when they're not willing to confront their sin before a Christ who's offering them another chance.

God wants to do something with whatever part of your life that's left.

God is a master rebuilder, and He wants to do that master rebuilding in your life because He wants to see you become what He created you to be.

You've got to be willing to be picked up by God, because you can't pick yourself up.

MAN UP

Use the following questions to discuss the video teaching.

Read the following verse together.

*When they got out on the land, they saw a charcoal
fire already laid and fish placed on it, and bread.*
JOHN 21:9

Jesus cooking breakfast. That's a sight I would like to have seen. The Savior of the universe stoking a charcoal fire, blowing on it to ignite the flame, and skinning the fish. This wasn't any ordinary breakfast either. This breakfast had an intentional purpose. The fish reminded Peter of his call to ministry years earlier: "Follow Me, and I will make you fishers of men" (Matt. 4:19). The charcoal reminded Peter of his failure when he denied Jesus three times, the last time while warming his hands over a charcoal fire (see John 18:18).

> **Why do you think Jesus chose to redeem Peter over a charcoal fire, a reminder of Peter's failure?**

> **Describe the lengths God will go to restore someone. How does that effort make you feel about your own future or the futures of people you love?**

When a construction company sets out to build a new skyscraper in an established part of a city, it often has to implode the existing structure to make room for the new. This removal of the past provides the space for a much more sound, artistic, and contemporary facility. God isn't afraid to tear down old patterns of thought, behaviors, and habits in a man in order to make room for His purpose and destiny to thrive in him. God sees the end from the beginning, so He doesn't fixate on the mess in between (see Isa. 46:9-10).

> **How can a greater understanding of God's intended outcome help men persevere in the process of restructuring, rebuilding, and personal development?**

On the video Dr. Evans said, "God has a purpose for your life. He has a plan for your life, and yes, we messed it up a lot of times, but God knows how to rebuild. He's the ultimate Mr. Fixit because He can take what looks like nothing and make it something. He can take something that looks like it has no future and give it a future that a man never thought he could have."

How have you witnessed God's rebuilding and restoration in your life or in someone else's life?

I once had the privilege of preaching in the exact location where Peter preached his first sermon after Jesus restored him. It's called the Southern Steps in Israel, and there more than three thousand people put their faith in Jesus Christ in response to Peter's message. Standing where Peter stood reminded me of God's faithfulness to use us in spite of ourselves. Not all of us have publicly rejected Jesus as Peter did, but each man, in his own way, has marginalized Jesus either through words or actions at some point in time. Yet Jesus remains faithful to draw us back to Him when we repent.

What are some hindrances that prevent men from accepting Jesus' call to restoration and rebuilding after they've failed?

A false sense of pride and a spirit of self-sufficiency are the surest killers of future ministry, influence, and impact. Men, when you've failed, admit it. Acknowledge your sin to God and repent. He's in the business of rebuilding, but it starts with your honesty and sorrow over sin. Peter went on to do even greater ministry after he was restored than he ever did before. Now he relied on God's power rather than his own. His is a lesson for all of us.

How can our small group and church create a culture in which men feel free to acknowledge failure and seek God's restorative power? Give examples of ways we can invite honesty and hope into our relationships and our church environment.

PRAYER
Close the session with prayer.

Father, You have the power to restore and rebuild what has been
damaged or destroyed in our lives. We look to You to manifest
this power both in and through us in all areas where we need
Your help. Give us boldness and courage to fully live out
our purpose and calling for You. In Christ's name, amen.

HIT THE STREETS

You Might as Well Be Honest;
God Already Knows

Never measure your spiritual life by your neighbor. Never measure your spiritual walk by how well or how badly everyone else is doing. Some men want to say, "Well, at least I don't do what John does. I must be a better Christian than he is."

The moment we start thinking like that, pride will trip us up. Sometimes we lie even when we pray. It would be much better to go before God and say, "I think I like You" or even "I'm angry with You."

You might think you'd feel uncomfortable saying that. Would you feel more comfortable lying? Keep in mind that God won't sanction our theological lies.

If your world has imploded, don't go around saying, "Everything is fine," because it's not fine. If you've collapsed, you're not OK. If your life has caved in, you need more than the standard three-minute prayer: "Lord, thank You for this. Thank You for that. Bless me with this. Help me do that. In Jesus' name, amen."

God says, "I'm tired of that. That's not really the truth. Your family is falling apart. You've got a pornographic mind. You're not loving your wife. You love your career more than Me and more than your family. That's what I want to talk about. I want to talk about those hurts and those sins. I want to get down to the nitty-gritty. Do you really love Me?"

Some men are living an inauthentic, fake Christianity, while others are living a proud Christianity that says, "I'm better than those other guys." When you come clean with God, He can come clean with you. Here are three ways to be honest with God.

1. Come Clean with Jesus

You might as well be honest. God knows the truth anyhow. When you pray, reveal the truth. It will help you and God get on the same page faster.

2. Be Authentic

Superheroes exist in movies, not in everyday life. We all have struggles, doubts, and fears. We've all failed. An authentic relationship with God and with yourself will open you up to the divine help you need to live out the best version of yourself. Don't aim for superhero; aim for spiritual greatness. Only God can get you there.

3. Do What You Can

It's OK if you need to tell Jesus in prayer, "Lord, I don't know what to say." Remember that He knows your needs before you express them (see Matt. 6:8). Too many times we aim too high, and when we can't reach that goal, we quit. Admit where you are. Start there and do what you can. God will help you grow in time.

BIBLE STUDY 1
Double or Nothing

As men, many of us have been challenged by powerful sermons we've heard or men's conferences we've attended, and we've responded in a genuine way. We have good spiritual intentions, make well-meaning spiritual promises, and pray great spiritual vows, only to find we can't carry them out. Our lives may even implode when we try.

When our lives implode, many of us stop and sift through the rubble. Instead of looking to Christ and the redemption and forgiveness He offers, we turn our poor decisions over and over again in our mind and miss the fullness of life Jesus has for us.

Read the following words of Jesus and answer the questions.

> *I am the vine, you are the branches;*
> *he who abides in Me and I in him, he bears*
> *much fruit, for apart from Me you can do nothing.*
> JOHN 15:5

What did Jesus mean when He said to abide in Him?

What happens when we make abiding in Christ an ongoing part of our lives?

Abide means "to hang out with." That's it. When a branch abides in the vine, it remains connected to the vine. As soon as it's cut off, the branch stops producing fruit. Why? Because the source of its productivity was the vine. To hang out with or remain connected to Jesus Christ is the secret to your eternal significance and productivity.

Read Luke 22:31-34. Peter claimed he would remain with Jesus. However, he denied Jesus soon thereafter. What led Peter to deny Jesus?

What leads you to turn your back on Jesus, even momentarily?

Peter had every intention of staying true to Jesus when he told Him he would never deny Him. However, Peter lacked the humility he needed to truly abide in Christ. Pride separates us from an abiding relationship with Jesus because pride says we can do things on our own. Pride says we're stronger than we actually are. Pride dictates our schedules and determines our thoughts. Humility is the foundation of an abiding connection to Jesus. Humility admits, "I can do nothing without Jesus."

In what ways does humility motivate us to abide in Christ?

I understand Peter's attitude. That's a cultural man's attitude. We trust in our abilities, position, power, wisdom, and strength. But like Peter, we have to learn that lasting impact comes only through Christ in us. Some of us fail in big ways, as Peter did. Others fail in small ways. But we all have to learn the same lesson, no matter how the Teacher gets it across. That lesson is the necessity of depending on and abiding in Jesus Christ's position, ability, authority, power, wisdom, and strength instead of our own.

Once you learn that lesson, you'll no longer make excuses for what you can't do. Rather, like Peter when he later preached to thousands, you'll discover that God can use you in remarkable ways, even beyond what you hoped or thought possible.

If Peter had sought to intentionally abide with Jesus and trust in Him, how could His moment of failure have been different?

NO MORE EXCUSES

Read John 21:15-17. How did Jesus respond to Peter's failings? What might Jesus tell us when we fail?

Notice that when Jesus restored Peter, He didn't rehash Peter's sin and failings. He didn't sift through the rubble with Peter. If we're truly repentant, our sin is as far away from us as the east is from the west (see Ps. 103:12). Once Peter reconnected to Jesus and began abiding in Him, he understood that he was forgiven.

So it is with us. God takes the mess we made and starts building a new foundation on top of it. He cleans up the rubble and forgets it was ever there. When we stop and linger to look at broken pieces, we're taking a man-centered perspective on our sin. Jesus wants more for us. Abiding in Jesus fills us with joy. We'll never live in the joy He's given us if we're stuck admiring the rubble.

What changed about Peter's life when he understood that Jesus loved him and had completely forgiven him?

Read Acts 2:1-39. What changed about sulking, foot-in-his-mouth Peter between that breakfast with Jesus and the day of Pentecost?

The same Peter on the beach was the same Peter at Pentecost. Yes, the same Peter who so often put his foot in his mouth. The same Peter who kept messing up, made promises he couldn't keep, was afraid of what the Jews would say, was scared of going public with his faith, and actually denied the Lord.

Peter not only stood up, but he also spoke up. His sermon on the day of Pentecost brought three thousand people to faith in Christ. And listen to his very public confession:

Let all the house of Israel know for certain that God has made Him both Lord and Christ—this Jesus whom you crucified.
ACTS 2:36

Peter publicly reversed his failure. He had denied Jesus, but now he proclaimed Him. That's called a turnaround.

Read the following verse.

> *Instead of your shame you will have a double portion,*
> *And instead of humiliation they will*
> *   shout for joy over their portion.*
> *Therefore they will possess a double portion in their land,*
> *Everlasting joy will be theirs.*
> ISAIAH 61:7

What joy can we find when we stop sifting through the rubble? In what areas of your life do you need to stop looking through broken pieces and receive the wholeness Christ has promised you?

People use the phrase "Double or nothing" when trying to gamble away a debt. This phrase means the debt will either be canceled if the person wins the bet or doubled. God doesn't call you to gamble, but He asks you to live by faith in His promises. He offers you a double-or-nothing option. If you choose to repent of the failures and sins you've committed and serve Him in an honest, humble, abiding way, He will repay you double what you've lost. Or you can stick to your own strength and continue to reap nothing. It's your choice.

PRAY

Pray about anything in your life that may have been harmed by your failures, causing you to experience loss or lack. Ask God to give you a right heart aligned under Him, not a perfect heart but, as Jesus illustrated with Peter, an honest, authentic heart. Then ask Him to restore to you double or even more of what you've lost in the past.

NO MORE EXCUSES

BIBLE STUDY 2
Cock-a-Doodle-Do

Jesus told Peter the rooster would crow when he denied Jesus three times. After Peter heard the "Cock-a-doodle-do" and realized he had betrayed the Lord, he went away and hid, ashamed of what he had done.

Peter may have thought the rooster's crow signaled the final curtain on his ministerial life. But when do roosters crow? Roosters crow to indicate a brand-new day. Peter was about to get a brand-new opportunity, despite the fact that he had a worldly perspective and a disobedient spirit.

Read Jesus' words to Peter:

Simon, Simon, behold, Satan has demanded permission to sift you like wheat; but I have prayed for you, that your faith may not fail; and you, when once you have turned again, strengthen your brothers.
LUKE 22:31-32

What did Jesus promise to Peter once he had been restored?

Jesus prayed for Peter. Scripture tells us He also prays for us (see John 17:20-23). Do you know what would happen to us if Jesus weren't praying for us? Peter went very low, but he would have gone a lot lower if Jesus hadn't prayed for him. The same is true for us. None of us know how low we would go if Jesus' prayers didn't keep us from going there.

I don't know what your low point is, but you probably haven't done what Peter did, publicly renouncing any association with Jesus Christ. That's about as low as any man can go.

If there's hope for Peter, there's hope for you and me. If Jesus wouldn't let Peter use his failure as an excuse to walk away and forget it, he won't let us walk away from His purposes for our lives. God has something better for us than sifting through the rubble of a collapsed life.

Jesus prayed that Peter's faith wouldn't fail, and it didn't. Peter was able to be restored.

Jesus said after Peter's restoration, he would "strengthen his brothers" (Luke 22:32). What could God do with our failures if, instead of fixating on them, we used them to benefit others?

What are some ways men can strengthen their brothers?

Are you actively seeking ways to strengthen the men around you? If so, what are you doing? If not, what can you start doing?

Peter couldn't begin to strengthen his brothers until he first came clean with Jesus. Over the charcoal fire Peter had to admit to Jesus that he had failed. Peter wasn't a hero. He wasn't a superstar. When Peter humbly admitted to Jesus that he was a fallible man who was able to do only so much, Jesus recommissioned him.

Peter first had to come clean with Jesus. He had to be authentic. Then Jesus said, "I have a place for you. Feed My lambs." That's grace.

Peter was honest and told Jesus what Jesus already knew. Even if your world is broken, if you'll be authentic with God, He can use you, bless you, and guide you to do all the things you've wanted Him to do in and through you. He's faithful to forgive those who ask.

NO MORE EXCUSES

How does this account of Jesus' conversation with Peter give you courage to be honest with Him?

Read 1 John 1:9. Why is confession more valuable than sifting through rubble of past failures?

Restoration is available to us. All we have to do is ask. We don't have to live with the guilt and shame of a broken foundation. Jesus will begin rebuilding the moment we ask. If we confess, He's faithful to forgive and cleanse us from all unrighteousness. That's restoration. He closes the cracks in our foundation and makes it as good as new.

Have you failed Jesus lately? Don't let the failure keep you from running to Him. For all his failures, when Peter saw the resurrected Jesus from the boat, he jumped in the water and swam to greet Him (see John 21:7). No matter what you've done. You don't have to stay there. You can run to Jesus and accept His restoration and forgiveness.

Read 1 John 4:18. Who has the ability to give perfect love? What does God's perfect love do in our lives?

Only God loves perfectly. If you'll receive His love, He will remove the fear of failure, regrets, and inabilities, replacing them with His acceptance, grace, and mercy. This reality frees you to love and serve, abiding in Him as He develops more of His character in you each day. As that happens, He takes all of our experiences—the good, the bad, and the ugly—and turns them into a platform for ministry. He takes us and uses us to build His church and further His kingdom, just as He used Peter.

What would you pursue for God if you knew you couldn't fail?

Fear holds us back from living in full faith. How does the gospel of Christ—the truest expression of perfect love—remove fear and replace it with courage?

If God loved you so much that He gave His only Son so that you could go to heaven (see John 3:16), He loves you enough to forgive any failure or sin in your life. His love provides strength and courage to live boldly and to risk all for the advancement of His kingdom and glory on earth.

Is there a particular ministry that God could build on top of the rubble of your past? What might that look like?

PRAY

Ask God to give you a full realization of His love, the perfection of His gift to you. Come clean with God about your spiritual walk. He already knows. Receive His forgiveness and grace. Allow Him to build you up in His love and mercy, committed to looking ahead and no longer lingering in the rubble.

Week 7
NO MORE HALF STEPPING

START

Welcome to group session 7 of No More Excuses.

Last week as you saw the dangers of sifting through the rubble, you also saw that God can build a new foundation on top of sin and brokenness.

As you read about sifting through the rubble, what stories of redemption came to mind?

All in. God wants your entire commitment, dedication, focus, and effort. Ever heard of a professional athlete who shows up for only half of the practices all season long? Me either. That athlete would either be released or be reminded that giving his full effort is part of the deal. Giving our full effort to the advancement of God's kingdom agenda is part of our deal too. Far too many men offer God a half-stepping approach to spiritual development and then expect God to show up and secure the victories they need. It doesn't work that way.

What would happen if you did your job at only half the effort required?

What would happen to a professional sports team if its players showed up for only half of its practices?

If you want to be a man of great impact and spiritual significance, you need to go all in. Effort. Consistency. Dedication. Hard work. Diligence. These are the markers of a kingdom man who lives with no more excuses. Let's learn together what it means to go all in for God.

Ask someone to pray before watching the video teaching.

WATCH

SESSION 7 Video. *To access the teaching sessions, use the instructions in the back of your Bible study book.*

The missing key to seeing God move in the life of a man is surrender. It is when we place all of our strength at God's disposal. It is when we take all God has given us and place it under His control.

We will forever be giving excuses when we do not allow ourselves to be owned by the Master.

Holy: to be set apart as unique or special

God says, "Do not let this system that leaves Me out become the dominating influencer in your life as a man."

You can't think like the world thinks if you want to get what heaven has to offer.

Every day you get up, you've got to let God know He owns you.

We can't be the real deal unless we are really surrendered and we give God everything we have got. We allow our strength to be submitted to His direction. We allow Him to define our identity.

God will feel comfortable hanging out with you because He knows you are surrendered to Him.

If you will give God the key to your life, give Him ownership of your existence, put your strength under His supernatural control, get up every day and say, "Own me, God," He will invade your manhood and your masculinity.

MAN UP

Use the following questions to discuss the video teaching.

Read the following verse together.

> *I urge you, brethren, by the mercies of God, to present your bodies a living and holy sacrifice, acceptable to God, which is your spiritual service of worship.*
> ROMANS 12:1

When the Titanic struck the iceberg, one important tool was missing from the lookout crewman's possession—the binoculars. Without the binoculars the lookout crewman wasn't able to detect the iceberg and warn the captain of the upcoming danger in an adequate amount of time. As a result, when the ship struck ice, a hole was ripped open in its side, allowing water to enter and sink the massive vessel. One missing tool created a catastrophe. Similarly, when men seek to live their lives apart from the wisdom and security of full surrender to God, catastrophes ensue. Surrender allows each of us to live our lives in alignment with God's will.

Dr. Evans defined *surrender* as "placing all of our strength at God's disposal." How would you explain the concept of surrender in everyday, practical terms to a friend?

During Old Testament times the priests made regular animal sacrifices as acts of worship on behalf of the people. These sacrifices included the killing of an animal on an altar. In no situations did the animal die on the altar, only to get back up, hobble down, and head back out to pasture. Once dead, always dead.

Yet that's exactly what most of us do with our spiritual sacrifice of surrender to God. We crawl onto the altar and tell God we're fully His, only to return later to our own thoughts, ways, and desires. We crawl back down off the altar when we want to, only to hop back on it when it's convenient, when we attend church, or when we have a crisis in which we need God to intervene.

Why do we so often give half-hearted effort in our sacrifice to God?

When Paul instructs us to present our bodies as "a living and holy sacrifice," what percentage of our time, talents, and treasures is he talking about? Explain your answer.

On the video Dr. Evans said if you surrender, "you'll discover that [God] will invade your manhood and your masculinity at a level that will blow your natural mind as a man. And now you will be the man you need to be." In other words, God will show up and work in and through you to influence others for His kingdom purposes. Not only that, but you'll experience what it's like to fully actualize all you can and should be as a man who's surrendered to His plan for your life.

When has God shown you that His ways are far superior to your own?

Dr. Evans used the example of dishes that are set apart for special use. Unlike everyday dishes, these dishes sit in a cabinet or remain on display, awaiting a holiday or special guests before they're used. This example illustrates what it means to be holy and set apart by God for His special, unique purposes.

What are some ways men disqualify themselves from special use by God?

Many shortcomings disqualify us from God's use. First and foremost is a lack of surrender to His will and purposes for our lives. There's no such thing as half surrender. God has a great plan for you, but you hold the key to whether He will carry out that plan in your life. That key is called surrender.

What's one small step you can take this week to increase your level of surrender to God?

PRAYER
Close the session with prayer.

Father, in a world full selfishness, You ask us to surrender. You ask us to lay down our ambitions, dreams, and desires and to replace them with Yours. We want to do that, but at times it's hard. Will You guide us in the process of learning how to surrender more fully to You in every area of our lives? In Christ's name, amen.

HIT THE STREETS

The Blessings of Being All In

Jesus pronounced an eightfold blessing on people who live authentic, committed lives of faithfulness and obedience to Him (see Matt. 5:3-12). We call these blessings the Beatitudes. They arise from three distinct attitudes toward ourselves, God, and others. Let's look at all three.

1. A Proper Attitude toward Self

Kingdom men who are blessed by God maintain a proper attitude toward themselves. They're "poor in spirit" (v. 3). They recognize their complete dependence on God. To be poor in spirit is the opposite of being rich in pride. The happiness that comes to those who see their spiritual poverty is that "theirs is the kingdom of heaven" (v. 3). They're the ones who have their prayers answered, who see God intervene in life's circumstances, and who enjoy their Christian walk.

Kingdom men not only see themselves as poor in spirit but also mourn (see v. 4). When Peter was confronted with his sin, he broke down and wept (see Mark 14:72). When Paul recognized his sin, he cried out in spiritual pain (see Rom. 7:14-24). When we feel the pain of God over our sin, we experience His comfort.

2. A Proper Attitude toward God

Kingdom men are also meek, or gentle (see Matt. 5:5), and they "hunger and thirst for righteousness" (v. 6). Meekness isn't synonymous with weakness. The term referred to bringing wild horses under control. A trainer took an uncontrollable, rebellious horse and broke it to the bit and bridle. When the process was finished, the horse was said to be meek. The horse didn't lose its strength, but its strength was under the control of the trainer. The blessing for men who are meek or gentle is that "they shall inherit the earth" (v. 5). Only meek Christians will see God take the earth and make it work for their benefit.

Kingdom men also have a deep appetite for the priorities and purposes of God. The blessing God has for hungry and thirsty Christians is that "they shall be satisfied" (v. 6).

3. A Proper Attitude toward Others

Kingdom men who are blessed by God possess a proper attitude toward others. Men who are merciful (see v. 7) put grace into action. Just as God looked down and pitied us in our hopeless, sinful condition, we must also show pity to others. The blessing for givers of mercy is that they'll also be receivers of mercy. If we're too busy to help others, God will be, so to speak, too busy to help us.

Kingdom men are also "pure in heart" (v. 8). They don't have to edit their lives. With pure men, what you see is what you get. The blessing for the pure in heart is that "they shall see God" (v. 8). That is, they'll see God operating in their lives.

Kingdom men are also peacemakers (see v. 9). They pursue unity, not divisiveness. They seek to pull people together, not tear them apart. God will ensure a strong, vital testimony for men who keep "the unity of the Spirit in the bond of peace" (Eph. 4:3).

Finally, kingdom men are "persecuted for the sake of righteousness" (Matt. 5:10). The idea here is to look so much like Christ in our actions and attitudes that what happens to Christ happens to us and for the same reason it happened to Him. The blessing for men who are persecuted and insulted for identification with Christ is a great reward in heaven.

BIBLE STUDY 1

The Chicken and the Pig

A chicken and a pig were walking down the street one day and came to a grocery store. A sign in the window said, "Bacon and eggs needed." The chicken looked at the pig and said, "Let's help the grocer."

The pig responded, "You must be crazy. For you that's just a contribution, but for me that's a total commitment!"

That's the way a lot of men feel about kingdom life: "Hey, I don't mind contributing a little here and there. But let's not go overboard. Let's not go as far as total commitment." Total commitment to God and His kingdom sounds a little too risky for a lot of men, as if the kingdom life will cost them too much. So they give a part of themselves to Christ but hold back the rest in case kingdom life gets too demanding.

Read the following verses and answer the questions.

> *One of them, a lawyer, asked Him a question, testing Him,*
> *"Teacher, which is the great commandment in the Law?"*
> *And He said to him, "You shall love the Lord your God with*
> *all your heart, and with all your soul, and with all your*
> *mind." This is the great and foremost commandment. The*
> *second is like it, "You shall love your neighbor as yourself."*
> MATTHEW 22:35-39

What are some reasons we stop short of loving God with all our heart, soul, and mind?

List practical, everyday examples of loving God with all your heart, soul, and mind.

Which of these two commands do you find hardest to obey, loving God or loving other people? Explain your answer.

Paul calls us to offer ourselves as living sacrifices to God:

> *I urge you, brethren, by the mercies of God, to present your bodies a living and holy sacrifice, acceptable to God, which is your spiritual service of worship.*
> ROMANS 12:1

Paul is commanding whole-life devotion to God. By definition a sacrifice was killed, yet Paul calls us to remain living sacrifices. We're literally to be the walking dead. How is this possible? Paul's description of his own life offers insight:

> *I have been crucified with Christ; and it is no longer I who live, but Christ lives in me.*
> GALATIANS 2:20

Crucification was a painful and shameful way to die. It was the Roman way of making sure someone was fully dead. When Paul said he was "crucified with Christ," he meant His desires, goals, and preferences were dead and had been replaced with God's will for Him. God's goals had become Paul's goals. God's desires had become Paul's desires. The only life Paul had was the life of Christ. That's why no one could intimidate this man (see Phil. 1:21-24).

Think about your desires, goals, and preferences. Are any of them out of sync with God's desires, goals, and preferences for you? If so, what are they?

What would it look like to crucify your will in these areas to pursue Christ wholeheartedly?

NO MORE EXCUSES

Which of these desires, goals, and preferences would you be most tempted to hold on to even though you know it's outside God's plan?

Notice that Paul never wrote in Scripture, "If you want to be committed, go to church." Worship starts with the commitment of our lives, not with our church attendance or our small-group Bible study. Although we should go to church and participate in Bible studies, they, in and of themselves, don't fulfill our commitment of total sacrifice to the Lord. It's tragic that so many people worship God on Sunday or participate in small groups but ignore Him—or even worse, worship themselves—the rest of the week. When we're living sacrifices, every activity of our lives becomes an act of worship. To worship means to ascribe glory. It's what we think about, what we invest our time in, what we focus our lives on, and what we offer as attractive to others. Worship encompasses our whole lives. It isn't limited to Sundays.

When we refuse to give God all of ourselves, whom are we really worshiping? How does that reality change the way you think about your devotion to your own desires?

What are some ways we worship ourselves in our secular society?

How can we counter this trend to surrender to God's call to full life devotion?

The greatest men in the kingdom of God understand that life isn't all about them. We're on a team, and our owner is the Lord. We play for Him. We produce for Him. We create for Him. We invest effort for Him. After all, He owns us. He paid the price. He covers, protects, and provides. What better way to honor God than by giving Him everything we have?

The problem is that many of us have settled for half-hearted worship of God, which is actually fully devoted worship of ourselves. When we make ourselves the center of our lives, we miss out on the life God has for us. We make excuses and refuse to give God what He requires—all we are. In doing so, we settle for half a life. God has promised us a full, abundant life (see John 10:10), but to take hold of that life, we must surrender to Him.

How could a community of men like your small group help us remain fully devoted to God? Why do we need accountability?

Do any other men know the ways you struggle with half stepping? Do they have permission to speak into your life with honestly and clarity?

Commitment is contagious. When one athlete works harder in the gym or plays better on the field, the other players often improve their performance as well. We need others to help us walk the Christian life. Many men suffer because they force themselves to be on an island. God has given us community to pursue Him together. Take advantage of it.

What's one way you'll display deeper commitment to God this week?

PRAY

Ask God to show you any areas of your life in which you're holding back from full commitment to Him. Ask Him to give you the desire to surrender your heart, soul, and mind to Him and to do whatever it takes to lead you to that commitment.

BIBLE STUDY 2
Follow-Through

Follow-through is critical in many sports, such as baseball, tennis, and golf, as well as for the quarterback in football. Follow-through means continuing the motion all the way through to its full extent. If you follow through in baseball, the bat stays in contact with the ball for the longest possible period of time, thereby propelling the ball with greater force and accuracy. Home runs result from excellent follow-through, not from checked swings.

If we as men are going to stop half stepping and live with greater commitment to Christ, we need to understand the importance of follow-through. We need to grasp the importance of going to the full extent in our faith by expressing it in our actions.

Hebrews 11:6 says, "Without faith it is impossible to please [God]." To believe in what you can see requires no faith; it's right there in front of you. But to be convinced that what you can't see is real and to have as much confidence in its reality as you do in what you can see, hear, taste, touch, and smell is genuine faith. In other words, authentic faith is required for you to follow through with confidence on your commitment to God.

Read the following verses.

> *Faith, if it has no works, is dead, being by itself.*
> *But someone may well say, "You have faith and*
> *I have works; show me your faith without the*
> *works, and I will show you my faith by my works."*
> JAMES 2:17-18

Why must faith be accompanied by action to be genuine faith?

Many baseball players walk up to the plate and point to the outfield, signifying a prediction of things to come. The player is trying to intimidate the pitcher by declaring that he's about to hit a home run. He may be seeking to convince himself of it as well. Athletes routinely visualize success prior to taking the field, hill, or track.

Many athletes visualize success, but so does a ten-year-old boy playing football in the backyard. Fewer achieve success. Like sports, faith requires follow-through. Visualization isn't a bad thing. God uses our desires to call us into action. However, if all we ever do is imagine all the things we're going to do for God but never actually do them, we're half stepping our way through our faith journey. God isn't interested in our half-hearted intentions. Faith requires action; anything less is disobedience. This principle isn't limited to our lives at church. It extends to our homes and offices as well.

Take an inventory of your faith-based actions. On a scale of 1 to 10, what level of follow-through are you living out with regard to your faith?

0   1   2   3   4   5   6   7   8   9   10
No follow-through   Complete follow-through

Have you ever replaced true obedience with a visualization of results? Why is this mistake easy to make? What keeps you from following through?

Is there a faith action you're visualizing right now? What would be required to put it into practice? What steps could you take this week?

NO MORE EXCUSES

Can you identify an area in which you aren't following through as a husband or a father? What's one step you could take to correct your half stepping?

Consider your vocational life. What responsibilities require your follow-through?

The point of these question isn't to make you feel guilty but to call you to action. Consider them a nudge to get into the game. When men take what God is placing on their hearts and move that urge to action, the kingdom benefits. When men live out their greatness as husbands and fathers, our communities are stronger. When men give full-hearted effort in their work, they recognize that they're not working for people but for God (see Eph. 6:7).

The faith we're to exercise as Christians has to be more than talk. James illustrated the point this way:

> *If a brother or sister is without clothing and in need of daily food, and one of you says to them, "Go in peace, be warmed and be filled," and yet you do not give them what is necessary for their body, what use is that?*
> JAMES 2:15-16

The benefits of faith don't happen just because we say the right things but because we execute the right actions based on what we believe and say. If you're a defeated man today or if you aren't fully living out your greatness and destiny, maybe you suffer from the problem many of James's readers suffered from: theology without practice. As James argued, that kind of faith is useless to God.

Describe a time when you acted with complete follow-through on something you spoke about with great faith. What were the results?

Based on today's study, record one step you plan to take today.

Follow-through ushers men into the type of kingdom impact God has called us to make. Imagine that you owned a professional baseball team and had a player who you knew could hit the ball. You chose to pay a high price for this player, but when you hired him, he chose not to hit the ball. Would you be pleased? What if he chose never to swing? That player would soon be off the team.

God doesn't kick us off His eternal team; salvation comes with eternal security. However, He limits His use of us in His kingdom program when we refuse to walk by faith with complete follow-through in our actions. No one would question a coach who benched a player who never swung at a ball. Similarly, we shouldn't question God when He chooses to use others who demonstrate greater faith through their actions.

PRAY

Read Psalm 90:17 and ask God to clarify the kingdom work He wants you to do. Invite Him to increase your faith as you take steps to obey Him. You may want to record the steps you take, along with ways you see God respond to your actions. Use your testimony to spur yourself to action on days when you doubt and to inspire other men to move out in obedience to God's call.

Week 8

NO MORE STANDING ON THE SIDELINES

START

Welcome to group session 8 of No More Excuses.

As we head into this final week, let's think about how far we've come.

You've made it to the final week. What has been the most impactful lesson you've learned from this study?

Named the Super Bowl MVP for Super Bowl 52, Nick Foles had done what few could during the Patriots dynasty: win a Super Bowl championship against them. Even so, the Philadelphia Eagles chose to keep him on the sidelines for the next season. After all, he was the backup quarterback. And even as a Super Bowl winner, he remained that.

But in week 14 the Eagles' starting quarterback, Carston Wentz, tore his ACL. The season hadn't looked great for the team up until that point. They carried a losing record into the next week's game against arguably the strongest team in football, the Rams. Few had hopes of a win. But Foles achieved just that.

What's one reason men become content on the sidelines of life?

Even though the season was an eventual loss, it ended on a strong note, and many believe it's because one man moved from standing on the sidelines to participating on the field.

Men, God has a plan for you. You don't belong on the sidelines. This week we're going to look at how you can take part in everything God intended for you to do by fully engaging on the field of your life.

Ask someone to pray before watching the video teaching.

WATCH

SESSION 8 Video. *To access the teaching sessions, use the instructions in the back of your Bible study book.*

No more excuses. No more living an ordinary life. No more sitting on the sidelines.

Nehemiah became a man of faith, influence, perseverance, dedication, unwilling to compromise.

You are the one to see the rebuilding of the culture.

Nehemiah didn't make the distinction between sacred and secular. He was going to bring the spiritual into the secular.

There's a battle in the spiritual realm that's causing chaos in the physical realm.

You've been called to be a man of impact, not just be a man by nomenclature.

When the enemy rises up because he knows what will happen if you man up, you're going to experience God overriding what you didn't think could be overridden in your life.

I'm going to stand up for the divine principles of God, and I'm not going to give any more excuses.

MAN UP

Use the following questions to discuss the video teaching.

Read the following verse together.

*For this purpose also I labor, striving according
to His power, which mightily works within me.*
COLOSSIANS 1:29

Strive means "diligently pursue an outcome." It involves hard work. Persistence. Effort. Consistency. And a whole lot of just plain determination. In this passage Paul tells us that his striving was done in the power of Christ, which strongly worked in him. Through His strength Paul was able to accomplish more than he ever would have on his own.

When have you had to admit that you didn't have the strength necessary to complete a task? Who came to your aid?

In the video Dr. Evans summarized the plotline of the popular movie *The Matrix*, in which a computer programmer is called on to literally save the world. He has a choice to make. If he takes the red pill offered to him, which contains certain powers, as well as entrance into another reality, he will be positioned to carry out his larger destiny.

Neo, the computer programmer, knows there's power in the pill. He also knows that the man offering him the pill believes in him enough to offer it. The combined force of this knowledge gives him the courage to get off the sidelines and into the battle on the field. We too have a red pill—the blood of Christ that works powerfully in us and gives us the ability to accomplish what can be done only through Jesus' power.

What has Christ empowered you to do that you never could have done on your own?

How do we honor Jesus and the sacrifice He made on our behalf when we take hold of the power He gives us, get off the sidelines, and enter the game?

In what areas of your life is God calling you to get into the game?

Dr. Evans used the example of a bowler who wears the right shoes and has all the right moves but can't knock down pins to represent a believer who looks the part but lacks true spiritual power. Looking good doesn't automatically equate with leaving a legacy of positive impact. We men have all the necessary equipment. Jesus has given us all we need to make a game-changing impact. To do that, we have to leave the sidelines behind and play the game in His power.

Why do we settle for looking the part? How could the working of Christ's kingdom power make an impact in your spheres of influence?

Kingdom men understand that making a kingdom impact involves more than looking the part. God seeks a man who truly influences the people around him for the kingdom of God. He's looking for a man, like Nehemiah, who risks his life to build God's kingdom in the world. Nehemiah was a government worker, not someone we think of as being a spiritual giant. Yet when Nehemiah saw a God-sized problem, he took a risk and asked to be subbed into the game. God is looking for bold obedience. He's looking for a man, like you, who will follow Him wherever He leads you to go.

Legacies are built of small acts of greatness stacked on top of one another. What's one small act of greatness you can do this week for the kingdom of God?

PRAYER

Close the session with prayer.

Father, we want to make an impact. We want to be a part of Your team to lead this world to You. Help us get off the sidelines and start working toward the goals You've established for us to live out.

HIT THE STREETS
Three Keys to Positive Impact

Nehemiah had a tremendous impact on his entire nation at a critical time in history. His life modeled what it means to be a kingdom man. We can increase our positive impact for the kingdom of God when we seek to apply the following three spiritual qualities from Nehemiah's life.

1. A Man of Faith

To be a man of faith, you must have a bigger view of God than of your enemies. If you have a bigger view of your enemies, they'll control you. Wind can't move an iceberg because most of an iceberg is beneath the surface of the water. But the current can move an iceberg, even in the face of a fierce wind, because the pull of the current is stronger than the push of the wind. If the pull of God is stronger in our lives than the push of our enemies, God's influence will win out.

I've been intimidated at various times, especially when my life was being threatened. But if I ever allowed the threats of the enemy to control me, I would have quit my ministry a long time ago. If we're going to do anything of lasting value for God, we must be men of faith. Times will come when we need to take a stand together, man to man, shoulder to shoulder, as men who believe in God.

2. A Man of Justice

Nehemiah held the leaders of Jerusalem accountable for being men of honesty and justice. Then he reinforced the seriousness of the situation and the need to make things right. Nehemiah didn't let God's people get away with unjust business practices, with holding their brothers in slavery, and with the wealthy oppressing the poor.

Let's be honest with one another. Some of the deeds we as Christian men tolerate aren't even on the borderline. They're just wrong. If we're going to be men of godly impact, we must be men of justice like Nehemiah. We must practice justice, insist on it, and fight for it when necessary. The question we need to ask ourselves is, *What does God think?* not, *What will people think?*

3. A Man of Perseverance

If you want to make an impact, don't stop doing what God wants you to do. Don't give up the dream God gave you just because trouble shows up. Keep rebuilding. Don't let other people knock you off the wall. Too many of us hear the world say, "You can't make any difference. Don't even try. It's not worth the effort." Who says? I'll tell you who says. No one with any real authority. The problem is that we're listening to those voices rather than continuing the work.

Keep on going. Don't let people who have no spiritual perspective stop you. When you persevere in what God has called you to do, you have the opportunity to make an eternal impact.

BIBLE STUDY 1
God's Ways

Nehemiah was a Jew living in Persia as a servant of Artaxerxes, the king of Persia. He was a descendant of the Israelites who had been carried into captivity by the Babylonians, who were then conquered by Medo-Persia. Nehemiah had no personal history in Israel, but his heart was there because that's where God's people and God's heart were.

Nehemiah received a distressing report from his brother about conditions in Jerusalem:

> *The remnant there in the province who survived the captivity*
> *are in great distress and reproach, and the wall of Jerusalem*
> *is broken down and its gates are burned with fire.*
> NEHEMIAH 1:3

Nehemiah was crushed, not only for the sake of his people but also for the sake of his God, because he knew these conditions were a reproach to God's name.

Nehemiah didn't start pushing for a political solution. Nehemiah didn't try to get the right person in office, get the right laws passed, or get the right programs in place. Nehemiah knew better, so he immediately bowed before God with tears, prayer, and fasting (see v. 4). He also turned to God's Word for the right perspective on his problem.

If you want to be a man of impact, you don't start with political, social, or economic solutions, although all three of these eventually came into play in Nehemiah's case. Rather, you fall before God in fasting and prayer, and you go to the Word.

Read the following verses and record the common element in all of them.

Ezra 8:21

Esther 4:16

Daniel 9:3

Jonah 3:5

Matthew 4:1-2

Matthew 17:20-21

Acts 9:8-9

Acts 13:2-3

Fasting and prayer are recurring themes throughout Scripture, particularly when an individual or a group of people were seeking to make a large impact on an entire culture or to carry out a mission of healing or service for God. When we get called into the game from the sidelines, fasting and prayer make up our first play.

Does fasting always have to mean abstaining from food? From what other activities can we fast in order to focus on seeking God?

Fasting is the reduction or removal of something that brings physical gratification as you seek God for a greater spiritual need. The temporary deprivation of something enjoyable helps us focus our attention on something better. Fasting is a means God uses to open our hearts and minds to the work He has for us.

Fasting isn't something you do casually. You can't just skip a meal or a TV show and call it a fast. Nehemiah wept as he fasted. Many biblical examples of fasting involved a contrite spirit. In relinquishing the power and attachment to the flesh, we let God know we're serious. Our full attention, surrender, and sacrifice can then be devoted to entering God's presence and crying out to Him.

Prayer and fasting allow us to hear the Lord more clearly, but you have to make time for them. Over the next few weeks, when will you take the time to pray and fast? What will you fast from?

NO MORE EXCUSES

Nehemiah fasted and prayed because the walls of Jerusalem had been torn down in battle. As a result, the city couldn't be safe and secure. Through fasting and prayer God led Nehemiah to action. However, Nehemiah mourned over the condition of the walls because he believed Jerusalem was the Lord's city that was meant to reflect His leadership and rule. To Nehemiah, the glory of the Lord was at stake.

Whatever walls are broken down in your life, your first action should be turning to God. Through prayer, fasting, and the Word, He will bring to your heart and mind the steps you must take to rebuild what has been destroyed.

Read Nehemiah 2:1-5. What did God lead Nehemiah to do about the condition of his fellow Israelites and their city?

God placed Nehemiah in the king's service. Think about where God has placed you. How could you be used for His service in those places?

Read Isaiah 58:8-9. How does God's larger perspective give Him a different vantage point for viewing our situation?

God has placed you where you are for a reason. Just as He placed Esther in the kingdom "for such a time as this" (Esth. 4:14) in order to save her people from certain death, and just as He appointed Nehemiah as the cupbearer to the king (see Neh. 1:11), God has a reason He has placed you where you are. God is intentional. Never let what you see determine the way you feel about your significance.

We don't have the perspective to understand all God is doing in the world. We don't know what God will do with simple obedience. It's not clear to us what God will do when we share the gospel with a coworker or seek to serve the neighbor down the street. God will take those extra moments we give to our wives and children and multiply them. He takes our ordinary obedience and multiplies it for kingdom impact.

Players on the sidelines don't contribute to the game. In what ways have you been passive when God is calling you to be active? How could you make an impact if you got into the game?

Is there an area of life in which you need to hear from the Lord? When will you fast and pray specifically for this need?

Who could help hold you accountable to remain in the game now that you're off the sidelines?

God knows the end from the beginning (see Isa. 46:10). He knows the plan. He knows what play to call. He's got the winning strategies for both offense and defense. And He can take you where you need to go. But being led by God requires fully seeking Him with your whole heart through fasting and prayer. It requires demonstrating your trust in Him by following His directions for every area of your life. If you want to be a man who makes a kingdom impact, then suit up. Get in the game. Play by His rules. His calls. And pursue His goals. His way.

PRAY

Pray about ways you can make a greater impact for the kingdom of God. Seek to be faithful where He has placed you and ask Him to burden your heart in the specific areas where He wants you to make an even greater impact for Him.

BIBLE STUDY 2
Leaders Leave Legacies

A man of impact is a man who takes spiritual leadership. I didn't say it's a man who wants spiritual leadership. I didn't say it's a man who talks about spiritual leadership. I didn't even say it's a man who studies the subject of spiritual leadership.

A man of impact is a man who *takes* spiritual leadership. He does it. He doesn't wait around for someone else to appoint him, ask him, anoint him, or nudge him. He just does it. He leads, and he leads well.

I regularly challenge the men of our church by asking them, "When was the last time you led a Bible study with your family? When was the last time you got on your knees with your kids? When was the last time you reviewed the Sunday sermon or a passage of Scripture with your wife, coworkers, parents, or friends and talked about what they learned or what they didn't understand?"

Men, you don't have to be a preacher to take spiritual leadership. You don't need a seminary degree to pray with somebody. You just need to do it.

Read the following verse.

> *Ezra had set his heart to study the law of the LORD and to practice it, and to teach His statutes and ordinances in Israel.*
> EZRA 7:10

List the three actions Ezra committed to take as a leader.

1.

2.

3.

First Ezra studied what God said in His Word, as you've been doing through this Bible study. Then Ezra went a step further by applying what he had learned to his life. He practiced the principles from God's Word. He put the truths to work. Then he taught them to others. Study, practice, teach. It's as simple and straightforward as that.

Why is it important to practice what you study before you teach it to others?

Have you ever tried to teach something without having put it into practice in your life? What was the result?

Have you ever known someone who lived what they taught? What impact did that example make on you? What would it look like to imitate this person's faith (see Heb. 13:7)?

Simply put, a leader is someone who knows the way, goes the way, and shows the way. The crisis today is that too many men are being defeated by, not delivered through, life's problems. The reason they're being defeated is that they don't know the Word, they don't know how to apply the Word, or they choose not to put into action what they know.

Jesus assigned each of us the role of teaching truth when He gave the Great Commission (see Matt. 28:19-20). He called us to make disciples and teach the truth of God's Word as we go through our everyday lives. This isn't a suggestion but a calling on the lives of all Christian men.

When was the most recent time you tried to explain Scripture to someone else?

NO MORE EXCUSES

Read 2 Timothy 2:1-2. Who's investing in you as a kingdom man? Whom are you currently seeking to train as a kingdom man?

Leadership is a lifestyle. It expresses itself in everything you do. It shows up in the way you handle success and in the way you handle defeat. Leadership involves applying all of the kingdom principles and biblical teachings you've examined in this study. It takes effort. Dedication. Desire. Consistency. Service. Sacrifice. Surrender. And a whole lot more.

What are the needs of your church? How are you involved in meeting them?

What skills do you possess that God could put to use in the church?

Take a look at your life. Identify areas in which you're making the greatest impact and look for ways to strengthen those areas. Then identify ways you could make an even greater impact.

Greatest Impact	More Impact Needed

In 1989 I was hospitalized when the doctor thought a lump I had was cancer. The night before the surgery as I lay on that hospital bed, do you think I worried about what other people thought about me at work or what kind of car I was driving? Do you think I lay there wishing I had the newest shoes, more friends, or a larger auditorium in which to preach? No, I didn't worry about any of that. What I wanted was the opportunity to live longer so that I could make an impact for God. I wanted to influence my children. I wanted to care for my wife in such a way that she could flourish in her career and interests. I wanted the people around me to be transformed by spiritual truths and the messages God placed on my heart each week to reach as many people as possible.

The lump wasn't cancer, and God gave me more years to serve Him. Yet as I enter the final season of my life, having preached for fifty years, I want to leave a legacy of impact for the kingdom. I'm sure you do too. Leaders leave legacies. It's what we do. You've been called to God's kingdom for such a time as this—to leave an impact for His glory, others' blessing, and the advancement of His agenda on earth.

PRAY

Record a prayer to God in your own words, asking Him to develop
you into the spiritual leader He wants you to be. Pray it daily.

Dear God,

_____

_____

_____

_____

_____

_____

_____

NO MORE EXCUSES

D-GROUP GUIDE

If you're reading this, you likely care about discipleship. You desire to be a kingdom man living under God's kingdom agenda. Being in a small group or a Sunday School class is one means believers use to go deeper in the Christian life. However, increasingly, people want closer and more tight-knit community. To this end we've provided a guide to facilitate those kinds of small groups.

WHAT IS A D-GROUP? As opposed to an open small group or a Sunday School class (meaning everyone is welcome), a D-Group is a closed group that three or four people join by invitation and commitment.

WHAT'S THE PURPOSE OF A D-GROUP? These groups are for Christians who desire to walk more closely with the Lord. The smaller nature of the group allows a more concentrated level of accountability and opens up discussions that are more personal than in a standard group meeting.

WHY DO I NEED A D-GROUP? We're not meant to live the Christian life alone. You'll need support as you seek to live as a kingdom man. Opening yourself up to people in a smaller environment encourages participation from you and from those who may not feel comfortable opening up in a larger group.

Additionally, D-Groups give others permission to speak into your life for encouragement, accountability, and prayer.

WHAT'S REQUIRED OF ME? The goal of these groups is deeper discipleship and accountability. Achieving this goal requires commitment. Plan to meet for one hour. Be willing to attend and participate each week. Be willing to be open and honest about your spiritual condition and about ways you're struggling. Be willing to hold what's said in the group in confidence. What's said should remain in the group as a means of building trust with one another. Finally, be willing to pray and support one another. Allow the relationships to extend beyond the group meeting itself.

How to Use These Guides

A D-Group guide is provided for each week of this study. These guides are meant to be used in addition to the weekly group session but can be also used by people who aren't meeting with a group. However, these guides work best if participants have seen the week's video teaching by Dr. Evans. Each D-Group guide is two pages and includes the following elements.

ARTICLES. Dr. Evans's sons—**Jonathan Evans,** a speaker, an author, and a chaplain for the Dallas Cowboys, and **Anthony Evans,** an author, a musician, and a worship leader—have written articles about the weeks' topics. These short devotional thoughts are intended to lead into a time of discussion.

D-GROUP QUESTIONS. In addition to the article, a passage of Scripture with some commentary and three questions are provided. These open-ended questions are designed to encourage men to open up about their struggles and successes for the purposes of growth and accountability.

Session 1

NO MORE HIDING BEHIND THE PAST

ANTHONY EVANS

Of the four Evans kids I'm the emotional one. I'm the guy whose feelings about the past can get so completely out of control that just thinking about my future wrecks me. In my most difficult moments, when I couldn't seem to figure out a way to move past where I'd been and the situations I'd sometimes created for myself, I would sit down with my father. He would remind me that our enemy's goal is to have us looking in the rearview mirror of our lives so much that we forget to look forward out of life's windshield.

There's nothing innately wrong with glancing in the rearview mirror to get perspective on what's behind; the past can help us make better decisions. But if we look in the rearview mirror too long, we fail to pay attention to what's happening now, and we set ourselves up for hazardous situations.

That lesson has always stuck with me as a constant reminder of the perspective we should have as men of God. There's a specific reason your rearview mirror is much smaller than your windshield. It's simply because where you're going is so much bigger than where you've been.

Glory Days Are Ahead

The past is can be a funny thing for guys. Many of us have a tendency to look back to our glory days. Maybe that's high school, college, or the beginning of your marriage before the hardships of later life hit you. The problem with glory days is that we look at them with rose-colored glasses, cutting out all that's painful.

Others of us look back at the past as a point of pain or sorrow. It could be the betrayal of a close friend, a significant loss, or a difficult obstacle. No matter how you see your past, a Christian's best days are in the future.

Consider the words of Paul, who had an eventful past:

Brethren, I do not regard myself as having laid hold of it yet; but one thing I do: forgetting what lies behind and reaching forward to what lies ahead, I press on toward the goal for the prize of the upward call of God in Christ Jesus.
PHILIPPIANS 3:13-14

What events in your past are you tempted to look at through rose-colored glasses? What do you look back on with hurt and frustration? How do these memories hinder progress in the present?

Why is it far more important for us to press on toward Christ? How are you doing that?

When are you most tempted to get stuck in the past? How can we help one another move forward in the present?

Session 2
NO MORE HOLDING BACK

ANTHONY EVANS

I recently became a homeowner. My dad was there during the home-buying process to answer all of my questions. Sometimes I had to ask myself whether the painful process of trying to prove to the bank that I could afford the house was worth it. It was more than annoying at times, but because I saw the property's value and had specific plans for what I wanted to do with it, I decided to push through. I walked through the house verbalizing and visualizing my plans, waiting for the moment when I could start executing them. I wanted to start the renovations as soon as possible, but I had to complete one task before I could begin. I had to go through the process of taking ownership before beginning the process of making a change.

A lot of us want to make and see changes in our lives without taking ownership of who we are as men of God. We hold back and wonder why we aren't able to truly lead and make changes in our home, church, or culture. I've had the privilege of watching my father make the conscious decision not to hold back and to take full ownership of who he was created to be. This conscious decision, although hard at times, led him to make permanent renovations in his character that made him the speaker, pastor, writer, and leader you know, as well as the father and mentor I'm honored to have.

I encourage you to take ownership of who God intends for you to be without holding back, knowing that ownership leads to the ability to make permanent change.

The God Who Doesn't Hold Back

He who did not spare His own Son, but delivered Him over for us all, how will He not also with Him freely give us all things?
ROMANS 8:32

God didn't withhold His Son from us, and through His Son He gives us all things. Why do we feel entitled to withhold from God?

In what ways are you most likely to hold back from God, your family, and your responsibilities? What causes you to do hold back in these ways?

In what ways do you need to be challenged to give more of yourself in service to God and others?

God gave what was most important to Him in order to secure our redemption. He didn't hold anything back but graciously allowed His Son to bear the shame and pain of crucifixion for us.

As we seek to follow Jesus, we hope that we become increasingly like Him, that His desires become our desires, that His thoughts become our thoughts. So we need to ask the question, Did Jesus hold anything back? No! Jesus gave His life in a world-changing act of grace and mercy.

Jesus took full ownership of the mission God placed before Him. He embraced it and never looked back. If we want to be like Jesus, we won't hold back. Not in our mission. Not in our homes. Not in our lives. We're all in because Jesus is all in.

Session 3
NO MORE WEAK LEADERSHIP

ANTHONY EVANS

I fly a lot for work. At times it seems I'm in the air as much as I'm at home. I've always found it interesting that on a cloudy or rainy day when visibility is low, the pilots still know where they're going. They taxi to the end of the runway and effortlessly take off into a white mist, which from my perspective looks like a complete disaster waiting to happen. The one factor that brings relief to the anxiety I have when flying is knowing the pilots have access to an instrument panel and a communication system. In that moment when nothing is clear, I trust that the pilots aren't going to lean on their own understanding.

Good pilots aren't just going to fly the plane in a direction they feel is right. They refer to the panel and communicate with the people in the control tower who can see conditions more clearly. The pilots know they're responsible for hundreds of lives, as well as the reputation of an airline, so they don't just take their seats in the cockpit and fly by what they see. Even in good weather they take their seats and then make sure they're reading the gauges correctly. More important, they put on their headsets and make sure they're connected to ground control. Then they begin to fly according to what they're reading and the directions provided by the people who see the bigger picture. That's the only way they can accurately measure their real distance from disaster.

God wants men who are leaders not just because of a seat they've taken but because they take the instrument of His Word and begin to prepare for takeoff only when they're keenly listening to His voice. That's the definition of a true leader.

It's time for men to accept the full responsibility of leadership, understanding that God has entrusted lives and the spiritual well-being of others to our care.

Model Leadership

*Remember those who led you, who spoke
the word of God to you; and considering the
result of their conduct, imitate their faith.*
HEBREWS 13:7

The author of Hebrews charges us to remember those who you led you and those who spoke the Word of God to you. He invites you to examine their faith and their lives and put their example into practice in your own life.

In order not to be a weak leader, we need to have a strong leader as a model. The world looks to business executives, athletes, celebrities, and politicians for model leadership. Though some of these men might lead lives worthy of imitation, the Bible never includes such people as examples.

The Bible calls us to follow the examples of men of faith, those who lead humble and quiet lives. The leadership we're called to follow isn't flashy and may not win the praise of society. Men worthy of imitation are those who get up early to meet with God and who love and lead their wives and children in a sacrificial way. They're the ones who invest in the next generation, teaching young men what it means to be a man. They do their jobs with integrity and confidence. They lead in ways that the world might not notice but that the Bible commends.

In what ways do you exercise leadership? How would you rate your leadership in areas where God has given it to you?

Is there an area of leadership in which God is calling you to take charge? If so, what is it?

What are actions we can take to hold one another accountable for leading where we're called?

Session 4

NO MORE GOING THROUGH THE MOTIONS

ANTHONY EVANS

My father taught me the meaning of pursuing what I know I'm called to do, even when I don't feel like it. He introduced me to the concept that my feelings ultimately follow my feet. What I mean is that men are constantly tempted to enter a place of complacency and just settle because the work required to be exceptional can seem daunting. What we forget is that it's often only after we reach the other side, after the pain of pushing through the mundane, that we truly experience the blessing of what God wants for us.

In most Bible stories there's a moment of the mundane before the miracle. Once we realize that remaining committed in the day to day ultimately lead us to the victory we desire, then and only then do our perspectives change about the challenges we're facing. As Ezekiel Elliott trains to be one the best running backs in the NFL, he runs the same route countless times to train himself to be a champion and to perform well under pressure. Serena Williams serves thousands of tennis balls to an empty court in order to be the best player in the world. If either of these athletes were simply going through the motions in their training, they would perform these drills, but they wouldn't develop the heart of a champion. Their attitude wouldn't be that of a winner.

Our hearts as believers should be willing to take our mundane moments and treat them as if God is teaching us truth about our victory, even if we don't feel it. When we believe we're going to win, our intention changes, ultimately affecting the impact of these moments. The result will be something we never could have imagined.

Push through Weariness

Perhaps you've heard the saying "Life is a marathon, not a sprint." While a sprint is quick work with quick results, a marathon is a slog. Running 26.2 miles takes commitment and dedication; it means pushing your body long after your body wants to quit. No one ever gets through a marathon by going through the motions. Distance running is a feat of endurance that requires you to keep going even when you're weary. It's an apt metaphor for life.

At times the daily routine gets to us, and we become weary. Weariness leads to complacency, and going through the motions becomes the default posture of our hearts. Those moments require an active choice to remain engaged. Going through the motions will keep you moving, but it won't get you very far. Consider this wisdom from Paul:

> *Let us not lose heart in doing good, for in due*
> *time we will reap if we do not grow weary.*
> GALATIANS 6:7

Doing good means living as God has planned for those who are called to follow Him. Christian men don't go through the motions. They give Christ-honoring attention and effort to all they do, not in attempt to earn God's favor but to demonstrate that they love Jesus and take their mission as seriously as He does.

In what ways are you merely going through the motions? What weariness led you to this point?

What are a few key steps you can take to reengage with God's purpose? How will you evaluate your new engagement level?

Who has been in a situation similar to you? What could you learn from their refusal to go through the motions?

Session 5

NO MORE COMPROMISING YOUR INTEGRITY

JONATHAN EVANS

Once a year I take my family to the Baltimore Inner Harbor to have fun. On one occasion we saw a mannequin standing on a platform in the middle of the outdoor commons. The mannequin was dressed very colorfully, was painted from head to toe, and wore a big hat on its head. We were intrigued enough to take a closer look. As we got closer, I saw the mannequin blink. I realized at that moment it wasn't a mannequin at all. To have some fun, I decided I would do everything in my power to make the man laugh, move, or talk and break out of his stoic state. So I began to dance, tell jokes, and ask questions to make him move. However, no matter what I did, he wouldn't move. He was so focused on his responsibilities that all of my distractions seemed irrelevant.

At last a man walked onto the podium and touched the man on the shoulder. Immediately his fixed expression relaxed, and he took off his hat. Then the man who had walked onto the podium gave the former mannequin a check and said, "Job well done!" I realized the mannequin wasn't moved by my distractions because he was focused on his reward.

A lot of distractions in life try to make men move from integrity. Suffering, pain, depression, sickness, anxiety, fear, hatred, mourning, career, and temptation can try to knock us off-kilter. However, we're called to stay focused on God instead of all of the circumstances dancing around us. Although distractions will always swirl around our atmosphere, God has instructed us in His Word to be steadfast and immovable on the podium of life (see 1 Cor. 15:58). If we hold still in His Word, a day will come when God taps us on the shoulder and says, "Job well done!" In spite of the constant distractions in life, we're called to stay focused on the One who holds our reward in His hands. Think about it. Are you holding your ground on what you know to be true in spite of your circumstances?

Steadfast and Immovable

Thanks be to God, who gives us the victory through our Lord Jesus Christ. Therefore, my beloved brethren, be steadfast, immovable, always abounding in the work of the Lord, knowing that your toil is not in vain in the Lord.

1 CORINTHIANS 15:57-58

The apostle Paul always grounded direction for living in a larger truth. In 1 Corinthians 15 he wrote about the resurrection of Jesus and its effects on our lives and witness. The previous verses are the culmination of this great discourse. Paul's conclusion is simple. In light of the victory Jesus has given us, we must live our lives doing the Lord's work, knowing that living this way isn't in vain.

Brothers, live with integrity because Jesus died and rose again for you. Refuse to indulge the passion of your flesh. Don't cling to the ways of the world. Instead, trust in Christ, who has prepared good works for you to walk in beforehand (see Eph. 2:10). Know that the Holy Spirit empowers you in your weakness (see Rom. 8:26). Trust that when you're tempted, you have a way out (see 1 Cor. 10:13). Live with integrity because Christ has empowered you to live that way.

When are you most tempted to compromise your integrity? How do you hold fast in those moments?

Why might sharing an area in which you're prone to sin with a trusted group of friends be freeing? Are there any sins you would like to confess today so that we can pray together and help one another?

What verses of Scripture could we memorize to help us when we're tempted to compromise?

Session 6

NO MORE SIFTING THROUGH THE RUBBLE

JONATHAN EVANS

In college one of my hobbies was breeding pit bulls. Pit bulls are my favorite breed of dog because of their strength; size; athleticism; and most of all, the size of their heads. The head of the pit bull is the breed's major selling point.

One day I was working in my home when I heard whining in the backyard. It sounded as if one of my dogs were badly injured. When I got out back, I found that one of my dogs was trying to escape. He couldn't jump over my six-foot fence, so he had decided to go under. The problem was, he didn't take into consideration the size of his head. He was stuck underneath the fence because his head was too big to go all the way through. One half of his head was outside the fence, and the other half of his head was on my side of the fence. This dog was as stuck as stuck could be. When he decided to escape from my presence and operate on his own, it proved to be a decision that got him stuck in a situation he couldn't get himself out of. There was nothing left for him to do other than call on the one from whom he was trying to escape to deliver him. My dog's greatest selling point became his greatest hindrance.

Sometimes the size of a man's head gets us stuck in situations we can't get ourselves out of. We can become so confident that our great selling points become our great hindrances. God is calling us to stay in the yard of humility so that we don't get stuck in the spiritual rut of self-sufficiency. Our greatest selling point as men must be that we trust our Master and be willing to serve where He has placed us to rule.

Think about it. Are you living your life with an oversized head?

Not Worth Comparing

We do not lose heart, but though our outer man is decaying, yet our inner man is being renewed day by day. For momentary, light affliction is producing for us an eternal weight of glory far beyond all comparison, while we look not at the things which are seen, but at the things which are not seen; for the things which are seen are temporal, but the things which are not seen are eternal.

2 CORINTHIANS 4:16-18

Paul was a man who experienced a lot of hardship. Before he met Jesus, he persecuted the church and tried to destroy it. After he met Jesus, he was beaten, arrested, met with suspicion, ridiculed, and shipwrecked. Interestingly, we never see Paul fixate on those moments.

Sure, he mentioned them when he was sharing the faith but never in a "Woe is me" way. His previous sin and his current hardship never caused him to take his eyes off Jesus. He acknowledged that we live in a sinful world that chips away at us day after day. However, he confidently said the rubble of this present life isn't worth comparing to the glory ahead.

If we focus on the rubble in life, we'll never see what Christ is building on a new foundation. Instead, we lift our eyes to what awaits us in eternity and focus on the men Christ is making us to be. We lay the rubble aside and focus on Jesus and the life He's preparing for us.

How can you use your past hurts to lead others to see Jesus more clearly?

Are you stuck in the rubble right now? How can you trust Christ's sufficiency to move through it?

Who is someone you can help climb out of the rubble?

Session 7

NO MORE HALF STEPPING

JONATHAN EVANS

You might not believe this, but the first time I dunked the basketball, I was only eleven years old. I know what you're thinking: *There's no way you dunked at eleven years old.* My father was thinking the same thing the day I ran into his office and shouted, "I dunked! I dunked! Come to the gym with me so that I can show you!"

When we got to the gym, I grabbed the basketball and told my dad to stand back. I vividly remember taking a position just above the three-point line and starting my race toward the basket. I put everything I had into leaping up as high as I could, and in the blink of an eye, BOOM! At eleven years old I dunked with authority.

When I looked at my father, however, he didn't seem to be quite as impressed as I thought he would be. He suddenly left the gym, came back a few seconds later with the head custodian, and kindly ask him to raise the goal I had dunked on from six feet to ten feet. Then my dad looked at me and said, "Son, don't be satisfied that you dunked at six feet, because that's not the standard for basketball. When you're ready to dunk at the standard ten feet, then I'll be ready to watch." I learned a valuable lesson that day. Just because I dunked didn't mean I'd met the standard.

Many men think they're doing well just because they're dunking at a cultural standard of Christianity. However, living as a kingdom man and living as a cultural man are two totally different standards. Just because the culture agrees with you doesn't mean God does. Just because you're stepping up in the eyes of the culture doesn't mean you're not half stepping in the eyes of the Father. Therefore, if your goal is to make your Heavenly Father proud, you must raise the goal and dunk at a biblical standard even in a pagan culture. We've been called to be like Christ. Everything else is half stepping. Think about it. Is biblical living your standard, or are you satisfied with cultural dunking?

A Fixed Hope

Discipline yourself for the purpose of godliness; for bodily discipline is only of little profit, but godliness is profitable for all things, since it holds promise for the present life and also for the life to come. For it is for this we labor and strive, because we have fixed our hope on the living God, who is the Savior of all men, especially of believers.

1 TIMOTHY 4:7,9-10

Half stepping results from a lack of disciplined effort. Dallas Willard famously said, "Grace is not opposed to effort, it is opposed to earning."[1] Although it isn't possible to earn salvation from the Lord, we use effort to follow the Lord. Paul compared following the Lord to physical training. If someone wants to be healthy, they need to commit to exercise. If someone wants to be spiritually healthy, they must commit themselves to following the Lord.

Half stepping in our spiritual lives leads to half stepping everywhere else because all we do flows from our heart. We need to be men who take seriously the call to follow Jesus wherever He leads. To do this, we need to commit ourselves to reading God's Word, praying, fasting, serving, giving, and loving other people.

As we develop discipline in these areas, the desire to stop half stepping in other areas will follow because our thoughts and our lives will be transformed by a God who doesn't half step. Our fixed hope on Him keeps us from half stepping in other areas.

What spiritual practices help us fix our hope on Jesus? To what spiritual practice do you need to more fully commit?

What are you currently learning about what it means to follow Jesus? Why is it beneficial to discuss these ideas with other followers of Jesus?

Confess any areas in which you're half stepping. Ask God to strengthen your resolve to give your best effort in the places He has called you.

1. Dallas Willard, *The Great Omission* (New York: HarperSanFrancisco, 2006), 61.

Session 8

NO MORE STANDING ON THE SIDELINES

JONATHAN EVANS

A famous tightrope walker planned to walk a tightrope across Niagara Falls. People came from all over the world to watch this man take the walk of death across the falls on a small rope. When he got on the rope and walked across with no problem, the people cheered in awe at this amazing feat.

Then the man asked the crowd if they thought he could roll a barrel on a rope across the falls. All of the people cheered and said, "Yes! Yes! We know you can do it!" The man responded by saying, "Then who wants to get in the barrel?" The crowd immediately went from cheers to absolute silence. Everyone looked around, waiting to see who would have the courage to put their life at risk. However, no one spoke up and came forward. Although everyone believed as a spectator, no one was willing to believe as a participant.

The Gospels depict the deeds of a perfect liferope walker named Jesus Christ. People came from afar to witness the miraculous works He was doing—healing the sick, giving sight to the blind, opening the ears of the deaf, casting out demons, and perfectly fulfilling biblical prophecy. People crowded around and cheered at the site of this incredible man.

Even in the twenty-first century, people are still crowding by the millions to celebrate Jesus Christ. In churches all over the world, people come together Sunday after Sunday to pay homage to this incredible man. With great certainty we cheer the fact that He can save, bring freedom, and deliver. However, Christ is asking for more than cheers from His people. He wants us to take risks, take up our crosses, and deny ourselves to follow Him (see Matt. 16:24). Many men will cheer on Sunday, but few will risk losing their cultural identities to fully identify with Jesus Christ every day. Christ isn't looking for faith spectators. He's looking for faith participants. Think about it. Are you a spectator or a participant in God's kingdom agenda?

Follow Jesus

When you look at the life of Jesus, you see a man who sat still. Sure, He enjoyed meals with friends, rested, slept, and had a healthy life rhythm, but He was never passive. He involved Himself in people's lives. He healed, taught, fed, and admonished people. He spoke to outcasts. He ate with tax collectors and sinners. He comforted the family of a deceased friend. He gave His life for the sake of our salvation and for the glory of God.

Following Jesus isn't a life on the sidelines. It means denying yourself and following Him. Jesus put it this way:

> *If anyone wishes to come after Me, he must deny himself, and take up his cross and follow Me. For whoever wishes to save his life will lose it; but whoever loses his life for My sake will find it.*
> MATTHEW 16:24-25

Three simple instructions: deny yourself, take up His cross, follow Him. We live as men who have no interest but the interest of our Father in heaven. We embrace the cross of Christ as the center of our salvation and the guiding point of our lives. We follow Jesus wherever He leads. Men, Jesus will never lead you to stay on the sidelines. If you follow His voice, you'll always be in the game.

Where is Jesus leading you right now? Are you following Him?

In what ways are you sidelined? What needs to change? How can we hold one another accountable?

What's your most significant takeaway from this Bible study?

Tony EVANS
THE URBAN ALTERNATIVE

YOUR *Eternity* IS OUR *Priority*

At The Urban Alternative, eternity is our priority—for the individual, the family, the church and the nation. The 45-year teaching ministry of Tony Evans has allowed us to reach a world in need with:

The Alternative – Our flagship radio program brings hope and comfort to an audience of millions on over 1,300 radio outlets across the country.

tonyevans.org – Our library of teaching resources provides solid Bible teaching through the inspirational books and sermons of Tony Evans.

Tony Evans Training Center – Experience the adventure of God's Word with our online classroom, providing at-your-own-pace courses for your PC or mobile device.

Tony Evans app – Packed with audio and video clips, devotionals, Scripture readings and dozens of other tools, the mobile app provides inspiration on-the-go.

Explore God's kingdom today.
Live for more than the moment.

Live for *eternity.*

tonyevans.org

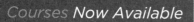

Also from
DR. TONY EVANS

U-TURNS
Reversing the
Consequences in Your Life

Learn to align your life choices
under God's Word and change
the direction of your life.
(6 sessions)

PATHWAYS
From Providence to Purpose

Use the biblical account of Esther
to discover your own pathway to
purpose as you learn and apply
principles of God's providence.
(6 sessions)

DETOURS
The Unpredictable Path
to Your Destiny

Find hope in understanding that
the sudden or seemingly endless
detours in life are God's way of
moving you from where you are
to where He wants you to be.
(6 sessions)

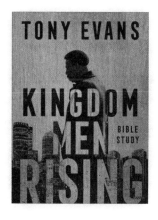

KINGDOM MEN RISING

Rise to the challenge of fulfilling God's purpose for masculinity. (8 sessions)

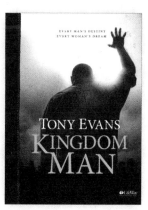

KINGDOM MAN
Every Man's Destiny,
Every Woman's Dream

Empower the men in your group with a Kingdom understanding, vision, and perspective on their identity and responsibilities. (6 sessions)

NO MORE EXCUSES
A 90-Day Devotional for Men

Inspire yourself daily with these short devotions to become the man God has called you to be.

Learn more at lifeway.com/tonyevans

Prices and availability subject to change without notice.

It's time for a change.

It's been said that if you always do what you always did, you'll always get what you always got. It's not certain who coined that phrase, yet few would argue with the logic behind it. A better tomorrow requires a different today.

Ever since the fall of Adam and Eve, life has been difficult. Destruction is easier than creation. Regressing is easier than progressing. Failure is easier than achievement. But despite the odds, some people find a way to make it. Why? Or, more importantly, how? This Bible study may not have all the answers, but it will give you a fundamental reason why so many people never accomplish what God has planned for them. Excuses. Through these eight sessions, you're going to find that the obstacles in your spiritual journey pale in comparison to the God who's walking alongside you.

- Learn from the examples of men in the Bible.
- Overcome setbacks and obstacles on the path to spiritual growth.
- See hard circumstances as opportunities for growth.
- Challenge yourself to be a man of character and commitment.
- Fight for purpose and meaning in your life.
- Lead with strength and godliness.
- Make decisions and take action while keeping your godly character intact.
- Commit to walk through life with other men who will point you to Jesus.

ADDITIONAL RESOURCES

DVD SET
005817574 $29.99

DIGITAL CONTENT
An *eBook* and video teaching sessions are available separately at lifeway.com/nomoreexcuses

Price and availability subject to change without notice.